Praise for Books by

# MICHAEL J. TOUGIAS

## EXTREME SURVIVAL: LESSONS FROM THOSE WHO HAVE TRIUMPHED AGAINST ALL ODDS

"If you're clinging to a lifeboat, surrounded by sharks (figuratively or literally), what should you think about? Who should you ignore? What are the patterns of mind and heart that have helped Antarctic explorers, soldiers, lobster fishermen, and prisoners of war stay sane—and alive? Michael Tougias converts the wisdom of survivors into advice we can all use to light up the darkness."

—Amanda Ripley, bestselling author of *The Unthinkable: Who Survives When Disaster Strikes—and Why*

"Each page is filled with the amazing arc of a human spirit exceeding all bounds, yet returning us, as readers, to what it means to be wholly human, humane, selfless, yet aware of one's self—call it identity, our authentic selves, a grasp of what's meaningful in one's life. Tougias' reporting and storytelling has appeal for armchair adventurers, historians of the extreme, for parents and families, teachers, civic leaders, those in business, and all of us in leadership positions large or small, who ask, 'How do I make the most of this moment?' "

—Doug Stanton, #1 *New York Times* bestselling author of *In Harm's Way* and *Horse Soldiers*

### THE FINEST HOURS: THE TRUE STORY OF THE U.S. COAST GUARD'S MOST DARING SEA RESCUE (COAUTHORED BY CASEY SHERMAN)

"A blockbuster account of tragedy at sea...gives a 'you-are-there' feel."

—*The Providence Journal*

"A gripping read!"

—James Bradley, author of *Flags of Our Fathers*

### OVERBOARD! A TRUE BLUE-WATER ODYSSEY OF DISASTER AND SURVIVAL

"A heart-pounding account of the storm that tore apart a forty-five-foot sailboat. Author Michael Tougias is the master of the weather-related disaster book."

—*The Boston Globe*

"*Overboard* is a beautiful story deserving of a good cry."

—*Gatehouse News Service*

"Tougias has a knack for weaving thoroughly absorbing stories— adventure fans need this one!"

—*Booklist*

### FATAL FORECAST: AN INCREDIBLE TRUE TALE OF DISASTER AND SURVIVAL AT SEA

"A passionately recounted peril-at-sea adventure...described with excruciating intensity. A blustery seafarer's delight, rendered with gusto."

—*Kirkus Reviews*

## A STORM TOO SOON

"By depicting the event from the perspective of both the rescued and the rescuers and focusing only on key moments and details, Tougias creates a suspenseful, tautly rendered story that leaves readers breathless but well-satisfied. Heart-pounding action for the avid armchair adventurer."

**—Kirkus Reviews**

"The riveting, meticulously researched *A Storm Too Soon* tells the true-life tale of an incredible rescue."

**—New York Post**

"Tougias deftly switches from heart-pounding details of the rescue to the personal stories of the boat's crew and those of the rescue team. The result is a well-researched and suspenseful read."

**—Publishers Weekly**

"Already a maven of maritime books with *Overboard!* and *Fatal Forecast*, Tougias cinches that title here. Working in the present tense, Tougias lets the story tell itself, and what a story! Anyone reading [*A Storm Too Soon*] will laud Tougias's success."

**—Providence Journal**

## RESCUE OF THE BOUNTY

"Tougias and Campbell superbly recreate the disastrous voyage, providing just the right amount of detail to bring every character involved in this dramatic tale to life, from *Bounty* captain Robin Walbridge and his shipmates to the brave Coast Guard rescue swimmers. A thrilling and perfectly paced book, *Rescue of the Bounty* is filled with good intentions but bad decisions, tall-ship history and current usage, and the roar and taste of the storm-whipped ocean."

—*Booklist*

"Riveting...breathtaking.... Tougias and Campbell build tension slowly and methodically...a sound strategy that pays off when they reach the storm itself. Then, the book becomes a white-knuckled, tragic adventure experienced by recognizable and sympathetic figures."

—*Richmond Times-Dispatch*

"A book that succeeds both as a high-seas adventure and as a psychological portrait of *Bounty's* ill-fated captain, Robin Walbridge...a gripping account."

—*The Day*

"A taut recounting of a needless maritime tragedy."

—*Kirkus Reviews*

"Tougias and Campbell's well researched and very personal effort details the doubts and questions as the ship gets underway, takes you aboard as the exhausted crew struggle to keep it afloat, then into the raging sea as the soggy survivors feverishly clamber into the bouncing rafts, and onto the tossing aircraft as the Coast Guard hoists the sailors from the maelstrom below."

—*Florida Times-Union*

## ABOVE & BEYOND

"The authors eloquently convey the difficulties and tensions involved in these U-2 flights, dramatically magnified during the crisis, when miscalculations could instigate a disastrous response by either side. This superbly written, tense, and sometimes sad account views the Cuban Missile Crisis from an unusual and telling perspective."

—*Booklist* (starred review)

"The authors have assembled a page-turning narrative.... Thinking of what a lesser commander-in-chief might have done, readers will shudder. An edifying history that, given America's current global diplomatic stance, is also timely and hopefully instructive to those faced with similarly dire circumstances."

—*Kirkus Reviews*

"The tick-tock narrative reanimates the drama. *Above & Beyond* documents the courage and skill of the U-2 pilots, one of whom was shot down over Cuba."

—*Wall Street Journal*

"A novelistic approach that involves dramatically recreated scenes and interweaving story lines.... The focus on two lesser-known figures gives the book an added dimension beyond other Cuban Missile Crisis histories.... [*Above & Beyond*] hums when describing the strategic maneuvering in Washington. The authors will leave readers with a greater appreciation of the work required to combat the 'miscalculations, incorrect interpretations, and breakdowns in command and control that could lead to war.'"

—*Publishers Weekly*

"A you-are-there retelling of the Cold War's scariest hours."

—*Military Times*

"Sherman and Tougias [coauthors, *The Finest Hours*] present an absorbing account of heroic U-2 pilots Rudolph Anderson [1927–63] and Charles Maultsby [1926–98] and their harrowing missions. The most fascinating chapters describe Anderson and Maultsby's lives, training, and assignments, especially Maultsby's catastrophic flight over the Arctic Circle that drifted into Soviet Union air space. VERDICT: Fascinating for general and informed audiences."

—Library Journal

## *SO CLOSE TO HOME*

"Through their meticulous research, Tougias and O'Leary take you where few historians dare, into the dark sea where an American family is floundering to stay alive, and onto the steel-planked deck of the German U-boat that put them there. This is priceless history, a fresh story in a modern era, and two hundred fast-paced pages of 'you-are-there.'"

—Adam Makos, New York Times bestselling author of<br>A Higher Call

"They don't come any better than Michael J. Tougias. His latest— *So Close to Home*—is a truly gripping, deeply affecting saga of undersea warfare and an extraordinary American family caught in the crosshairs of history."

—Alex Kershaw, New York Times bestselling author of<br>The Longest Winter and The Few

"A must-read, told from multiple points of view, about how WWII got a lot closer than most people think."

—NY Post

"Tougias's books dot the *New York Times* bestseller list, and now he has a dramatic new narrative."

—Worcester Telegram

"Tougias knows how to tell a story, especially real-life stories of survival."

—Gail McCarthy, Gloucester Daily Times

"Tougias and O'Leary impressively render the early period of US involvement in WWII. The Downs family...survival defied the odds."

*—Publishers Weekly*

"Compelling action and vivid character portrayals..."

*—Metro West Daily News*

"A unique perspective on the almost forgotten threat of Nazi U-boats in American waters."

*—Military.com*

"A gripping read..."

*—Herald Dispatch*

"This amazing story of U-boats will air on BBC World Service and be heard around the world as it deserves."

*—Daniel Gross, BBC*

"A gripping tale of family fortitude in the face of disaster. And the German side of the story is told in a manner sympathetic to commanders and crews who suffered in service of their country's flawed cause."

*—AuthorLink*

"A solid perspective of hardships endured by ordinary people."

*—Library Journal*

"An amazing and inspiring story of a family who survived against all odds."

*—National Examiner*

# EXTREME SURVIVAL

# EXTREME SURVIVAL

Lessons from Those Who Have
Triumphed Against All Odds

*NEW YORK TIMES* BESTSELLING AUTHOR

# MICHAEL J. TOUGIAS

mango
PUBLISHING GROUP
CORAL GABLES

Cover Design: Megan Werner
Cover Photo/illustration: BSANI / stock.adobe.com
Layout & Design: Megan Werner

For permission requests, please contact the publisher at:
Mango Publishing Group
2850 S Douglas Road, 4th Floor
Coral Gables, FL 33134 USA
info@mango.bz

For special orders, quantity sales, course adoptions and corporate sales,
please email the publisher at sales@mango.bz. For trade and wholesale
sales, please contact Ingram Publisher Services at customer.service@
ingramcontent.com or +1.800.509.4887.

Extreme Survival: Lessons from Those Who Have Triumphed Against
All Odds

Library of Congress Cataloging-in-Publication number: 2022942979
ISBN: (p) 978-1-68481-061-1 (e) 978-1-68481-062-8
BISAC category code SOC040000, SOCIAL SCIENCE / Disasters &
Disaster Relief

Printed in the United States of America

To my friend across the pond, George Roux,
and all the survivors who shared their insights

_____

# CONTENTS

INTRODUCTION

# INTRODUCTION

I've spent over thirty years writing books about amazing stories of survival, and my favorite part of the process was interviewing the survivors. I learned the details, not only of their harrowing ordeal, but also of how they eventually triumphed in face of overwhelming odds against them. They succeeded where the rest of us might think, *I could never have made it.*

For the most part, the people I interviewed survived experiences that lasted not just an hour or two, but several hours, or even days, where they faced a multitude of potentially life-ending threats. I began to think of these people as extreme survivors, and I was especially curious about the techniques they used to keep fighting and not give up. It also became apparent that these people made sound decisions, despite being under incredible pressure, and I wanted to understand how they stayed relatively calm in a whirlwind of chaos.

A few years ago I went through a difficult period in my life, and to help cope—and eventually overcome the challenge—I started thinking like the survivors I got to know. I emulated their mindsets, their outlooks, and the techniques they used to get to the other side of the survival situations they found themselves in. My personal circumstance certainly wasn't life-threatening, but it did feel overwhelming and demanded I make thoughtful decisions under duress. So in that sense there were similarities, and I found it helpful to adopt some of the same steps, attitudes, and even reactions that the survivors employed. That's when the idea for this book was born. I realized that there was a wealth of information to learn from people who make it to the other side of life's most daunting challenges.

For this book, I decided to use not only the survivors that I interviewed but also survivors who either wrote about their ordeals or were featured by other authors and writers. I read every survival book I could locate, and from those selected only the survivors who had had the most difficult trials to overcome. Although their individual experiences were quite different, I began to see common mindsets and techniques that were used. These patterns and commonalities became the core of the book.

The approach I use in the following pages is to first chronicle an individual's harrowing story, so that the reader is thrust into the situation and might think *What would I have done?* Then, after what I hope is an edge-of-your-seat read, I dive into the analysis of exactly how the survivors accomplished what would seem impossible for most of us. And finally, I relate how we can all use these techniques when faced with adversity or aspiring to achieve a difficult goal.

Most of the survivors I've personally worked with were involved in recent accidents at sea, so to broaden the appeal of the book, I researched individuals who faced challenges quite different than a punishing ocean. The stories I found the most compelling spanned centuries: historic epics which occurred from hundreds of years ago right up to the present—from early explorers of the New World, to survivors of Nazi concentration camps, to POWs in Vietnam, and airline pilots of today. The locations range from the South Pole, the Amazon, Yosemite's Half Dome, Mount Everest, Newfoundland, and the Rocky Mountains, to Iraq, the Andes Mountains, Kyrgyzstan, and the oceans of the world. A few stories are not set in remote places, but instead in New York City and a suburb outside Boston. The locations are as varied as the people involved.

Join me on this journey of courage, bravery, ingenuity, and persistence. I'm betting we all come away from the experience a little wiser and a little more confident in our own strengths.

CHAPTER 1

# THE POWER OF LITTLE STEPS & SURVIVORS' MINDSETS

"I might not make it, but I'm going to go down fighting."

—Ernie Hazard

"I'm going to take this as far as I can. Try to embrace the experience."

—Brad Cavanaugh

The five shipwreck survivors clinging to the eleven-foot inflatable Zodiac were in the trough of a thirty-foot swell and looked up into the green walls of water. That's when they saw the sharks.

Brad Cavanaugh, age twenty-one, could clearly see three sharks, and one was larger than the Zodiac. "It was bad enough seeing how large that shark was, but even worse was that the shark could clearly see us," Brad recalled.

This shark knew there was life inside the life raft, and it wasn't about to leave.

From the moment the sailboat he was on, named *Trashman*, sank, Brad made up his mind he was going to live. He thought of his mother and how his death would crush her, so he said to himself, *I'm going to take this as far as I can. And because this is now my world, my reality, I'm going to embrace it. I'm going to fight to the end.*

His reality was bleak, surviving was near impossible, and the world that he tried to embrace included four others—with very different thoughts—and Brad had to be cognizant of them in any decisions he made.

The *Trashman* had been sailing approximately sixty miles off North Carolina when a violent storm with 100 mile per hour winds and forty-foot seas sank the vessel at 1:30 p.m. on October 24, 1982. Brad, Deb, Mark, John, and Meg had just two minutes to leave the vessel before it dragged them to the ocean's depths. There were no survival suits onboard and no time to even put on life jackets: the crew had to escape with the clothes on their backs.

As their boat sank, Mark tried to free the life raft from its canister while Brad untied the rubber Zodiac dinghy from the *Trashman*'s cabin top. When the life raft popped from its canister and inflated it was taken by the wind and disappeared into the chaotic void of crashing seas. The Zodiac came free of the *Trashman* as the sailboat was going down, and it too was snatched by the wind and began tumbling away.

Brad knew that if he didn't corral the Zodiac, he and the rest of the crew were doomed, so he swam after it, kicking off his boots as he went. Somehow, he caught up with the tiny vessel and held onto its lifeline in the raging sea until the others could reach him. The group tried to hold onto to the outside of the Zodiac by clutching the lifeline, but the hurricane-force winds, coupled with breaking seas, sent the vessel rolling end over end. Some of the crew who were able to hang on were flipped with the dinghy while others lost their grip and had to swim after it.

They soon learned it was easier to keep the Zodiac from getting caught by the wind if they kept it upside down and held on to its outer edges. The wind and waves lashed the crew and they all ingested seawater, but at least the dinghy stayed in place.

About an hour into the ordeal, Brad was faced with the first of many crucial decisions that he had to convince the group to adopt. The air temperature was approximately fifty-four degrees Fahrenheit, but the survivors were not too cold as they continually treaded water and held the Zodiac snug to the ocean's surface to keep it from blowing away. John, the captain of the *Trashman*, thought they should turn the dinghy right-side up and get inside it. Brad was certain that if they righted the vessel the wind and waves would flip the dinghy and toss everyone into the ocean where they may not be able to retrieve the vessel. He shouted at John that the time was not right to get in the dinghy, but John was adamant. Fortunately, Brad and Deb had another idea, an option no one had considered yet: get under the Zodiac. This would protect them from the blasting wind, and by holding onto the lifeline, they wouldn't risk having the dinghy blown away.

As the group huddled beneath the Zodiac on the up-wind side, they all wondered when the Coast Guard would come. On the boat they had been in communication with the Coast Guard, telling them about the severity of the storm and how the sailboat was damaged and in jeopardy of sinking. The Coast Guard responded by sending a C-130 aircraft into the storm and that plane located the *Trashman*. A mechanical issue, however, forced the plane to turn back to Air Station Elizabeth City. Over the radio, Coast Guard Search and Rescue told John that two merchant ships were being diverted to the *Trashman* but would take several hours to arrive. The Coast Guard then asked John to return to the radio each hour and give them an update.

Now, with the boat at the bottom of the ocean and John missing that hourly update, the group wondered why another Coast Guard aircraft had not arrived on the scene. The survivors assumed that sooner or later the Coast Guard would come, but inexplicably that never happened. (Later, a lawsuit initiated by the castaways and/or family members against the Coast Guard was settled out of court.)

Four hours went by with the group huddled under the raft (Meg mostly stayed on the outside of the vessel because she was claustrophobic). They had been expending energy handling the *Trashman* before it sank, and now they were burning even more calories and strength treading water. All of the crew started shivering from their time in the water. Hypothermia was setting in, and a couple of the survivors' teeth were chattering so loudly the others could hear the clicking. Again, Brad and Deb came up with an idea to improve their situation. Using a wire salvaged from the overturned dinghy, Brad stretched it from one side to the other. He then put his legs over the wire, so that the wire supported his legs beneath the knee while his head and shoulders lay on the spray cover that extended over the dinghy's bow. Mark, Deb, and John crammed next to and on top of Brad, keeping part of their bodies out of the water and sharing body heat. Meg, who had serious leg lacerations, still stayed on the outside of the overturned Zodiac.

In the morning, as the wind eased and the seas didn't break as often, the group was able to turn the raft right-side up. Some were reluctant to get inside because the air felt so much colder than the water. But they changed their minds when Mark and Deb, who were outside the raft, looked down into the water and saw not one shark, but many!

All five castaways pulled themselves into the raft, which had floor space of only three feet wide by four feet long. There was not enough room to stretch out cramped legs, and each time one moved or bumped against another it caused pain because they all suffered from various abrasions that were now inflamed.

As the Zodiac rode a wave crest, Brad could see fins circling their vessel. In the trough, when he looked up into the wave, was when he saw the especially large shark looking back at him. The little vessel was still in jeopardy of being capsized by the enormous swells and Brad made it his job to be the "balancer" of the life raft. He would shift his body as needed, mostly by using his legs and butt. Yet still he was afraid the raft would flip and send them into the shark-infested water. His mind was churning, trying to think of some way to make sure the group stayed inside the Zodiac.

It was becoming clear to Brad that only he and Deb were thinking in terms of improving their situation. The others were showing signs of defeat. Talk of water and thirst were beginning to dominate discussions which Brad tried to shut out. He later explained to me, "I couldn't go there. Put that one away. There was nothing I could do about the lack of water."

Brad consciously tried to direct his thoughts away from what was out of his control, and instead be alert for an opportunity or an idea that he could consider and take action on. The very act of doing *something* helped keep him from dwelling on all the many depravations and pain. In essence, he was clinging to the one thing he could control and that was his reaction to what was happening to him.

Brad and Meg decided they would make a sea anchor to trail behind the raft to add stability. They used the same piece of wire they previously hung their legs on and attached it to a small piece of wood that they pried off a storage space in the bow. Once it was rigged, Brad hurled it behind the raft.

Almost immediately the raft was jerked backward. The big shark had grabbed the board!

Brad saw the shark take the board and just two seconds later release it. Mark quickly pulled the board in, and now the giant shark swam directly at the raft. Raising the board, Mark prepared to strike it.

"No!" Brad shouted, and he yanked the board from Mark's grasp. "Don't rile it up! It might attack the raft!"

Instead, the shark slowly slid beneath the Zodiac, its head on one side and its fin on the other. A shiver went through Brad as he could feel the beast rub against the floor of the raft.

*Goddamn, what else could go wrong*, thought Brad. *This is so bad, so utterly horrifyingly absurd, it's almost comical.* His idea to create a sea anchor was foiled by the shark. And later another idea to remove the thin aluminum sheet that covered the raft's floor failed as well, in fact it resulted in Brad cracking his teeth trying to free the sheets. But the most critical fact, however, was that Brad was still trying to better their situation. Both he and Deb were not done fighting, thinking, and hoping. In the hours to come—which eventually *stretched into four days*—that mindset, the continual process of taking little steps to try and improve their odds, was the number one reason they survived and the others did not.

The hallucinations occurred on the third day. Brad believes they were caused by the combination of exhaustion, dehydration, and hypothermia. Mark and John exacerbated their mental deterioration by sipping small amounts of seawater.

John soon became convinced they were just a few hundred yards off the coast of Falmouth, Massachusetts, and he began talking about getting his car. Although Brad had hallucinations, at this particular moment he was lucid, and he and Deb told John they were far out in the ocean, nowhere near the coast.

Suddenly, John acted on his plan, sliding over the side of the Zodiac. Brad and Meg shouted for him to get back in the dinghy, but John simply said, "I'm getting the car," and swam off.

Torn over whether to try and retrieve John, Brad soon realized it was a lost cause as John found the energy to stroke far from the raft. Then there was an awful scream.

Not long afterward, Mark started talking about going to the store because he needed cigarettes. "No," said Brad. "You're not going to the store. You're in a life raft and you're safe." That calmed Mark down for a while and Brad closed his eyes trying to conserve what little energy he had left.

Then Mark went over the side, saying "I'm going to 7-Eleven to buy cigarettes." The sharks yanked him under before he could even scream.

The sharks, now in a frenzy, set their sights on the raft, battering it from all sides. If one of the creatures bit down on the inflated rubber, it would be all over.

Brad, Deb, and Meg huddled together in fear and to share body heat. At this point there was little more Brad and Deb could do to help Meg or their situation. Earlier they had scooped seaweed from the ocean and covered themselves with it for insulation, but the cold was penetrating to their cores. Even Brad started thinking they had just hours to live rather than days.

Losing Mark and John was devastating to Brad. He explained how the hurt was not just the loss of his friends but also to his resolve to survive. "That opened the door for death to come into our raft. I felt if one of us died then we were inviting death in, and our focus would shift from living to dying."

As Brad lay in the raft and felt the sharks bumping it, he told himself over and over: *Don't give up. We've seen a couple ships in the distance, our luck is bound to change.*

Luck—really more like a miracle—is what Meg needed, but it never came, and she died that night. She likely expired from exhaustion and the infection that set into her wounds suffered while the sailboat was sinking. In the morning, Brad and Deb said a prayer over Meg's lifeless body and then released her to the sea.

Later in the day Brad was faced with another crucial decision. As there were no sharks in sight, Deb wanted to flip the Zodiac so that they could get the putrid water out of it. Brad worried the sharks were still nearby but unseen. He also knew that his strength was so low he may not be able to climb back in the dinghy [his weight on his 6'2" frame had dropped from 205 pounds to 165 pounds]. But Brad also considered that Deb had gone along with his ideas and how it was essential that they remain united. He ultimately agreed with Deb.

The consequences of the decision almost cost Brad his life. After they intentionally flipped the raft, cleaned it, and then put it right-side up, he labored to get out of the water and back in the Zodiac. Deb, whom Brad had helped push back into the raft, now struggled to pull Brad over the side.

They waited a moment, gathered all their strength and together maneuvered Brad into the vessel, where he collapsed and started vomiting. For the first time, Brad felt certain he would be dead within an hour. He simply had nothing left—nothing left physically that is. But mentally he wasn't quite ready to call it quits.

When he caught his breath, he managed to sit up and then talked with Deb about trying to catch fish. Earlier he had caught a very small fish with his bare hands, but it was nothing but skin and bones. He wasn't sure he could catch a larger fish, but he had to say something positive, to shut the door on the thought of his death.

Not long after cleaning the Zodiac, the luck that Brad and Deb so desperately needed came in the form of a Russian ship, which eventually saved them. Let me rephrase that: the ship's crew plucked them from the water, but what saved them was the power of little steps.

These two castaways made it largely because they kept focusing on the few things they could initiate, rather than let the despair they felt push them toward resignation. The fact that Brad and Deb kept thinking, experimenting, and attempting improvements—no matter how small—gave them a glimmer of achievement, and even a fleeting bit of control. *The message for all of us is to take those little steps that might seem insignificant when you feel helpless and string a few actions together. Before you know it, you have advanced toward your objective.*

As Brad explained his survival story to me, I was struck by the similarities in Brad's thinking and actions of another survivor I interviewed many years earlier and grew close to. That man was Ernie Hazard, who survived the sinking of his fishing vessel by an estimated 90- to 100-foot rogue wave. One comment Ernie made to me during our discussions sounded as if it could have come from Brad. Ernie summed up his mindset during his ordeal this way: "I might not make it, but I'm going to go down fighting."

Although Ernie's actions, attitude and determination were similar to Brad's, his story is important to tell because of one major difference. From the moment the wave hit to his ultimate survival three days later, Ernie was all alone. He offers us wisdom of how to overcome incredible odds when you have no one to talk to but yourself.

Ernie's saga began on a cold November day in 1980 when two fishing vessels, the *Fair Wind* and the *Sea Fever*, set out from Cape Cod, Massachusetts to catch offshore lobsters at Georges Bank, lying 130 miles to the southeast. On the day they departed, the weather reports forecast typical autumn conditions for the next three days on the fishing grounds. The National Weather Service issued this report even though the organization knew its lone weather buoy at Georges Bank was malfunctioning. The Weather Service also elected not to tell mariners of the malfunction.

When the *Sea Fever* and *Fair Wind* reached Georges Bank the next morning, the seas were building rapidly and the wind was approaching gale force. Over the course of the morning the waves built to sixty feet and both vessels were trapped on Georges Bank, miles from safe harbor.

The storm soon reached hurricane force with winds topping an incredible 100 miles per hour, and both vessels were in grave danger. Captain Peter Brown on the *Sea Fever* (his father owned the *Andrea Gail* of *Perfect Storm* fame) swung the boat around so it would face the seas and avoid having its stern driven under by the breaking waves. Suddenly, a monstrous wave broke over the bow and smashed its windshield, sending water flooding down to the bilge.

Peter recovered from the blow, shouted out a Mayday on the radio, then turned the boat downwind so that another wave would not cascade through the gaping hole. He handed the wheel to crewman Gary Brown (no relation) and shouted for the other crewmembers to start cutting plywood for the shattered windows. Peter then tied a rope around his waist in preparation of going out on the deck to install the plywood.

That's when an enormous wall of water hit the vessel. The force of the blow was so powerful it sent Gary Brown crashing through the wooden wall of the pilothouse and into the churning sea. The boat righted itself, but the engine conked out. While Peter Brown rushed below to restart the engine, the remaining two crewmembers ran to the stern where they saw Gary floating in the water, face up, about fifteen feet away. They repeatedly threw a line to Gary, but the floating crewman was either in shock or unconscious, and he made no attempt to grab the lifeline. More huge waves battered the boat, sending it careening sideways into the valleys between the seas. For the next twelve hours, the three remaining crewmen were in the fight of their lives, trying to outlast this incredible storm.

On board the second boat, the *Fair Wind*, Captain Billy Garnos, first mate Ernie Hazard and two crewmembers were also struggling to stay afloat in rampaging seas. The same enormous wave that hit the *Sea Fever* came at their boat, and Garnos gave the vessel full throttle to climb the ninety-foot monster. The *Fair Wind*, however, was no match for the wall of water, and the vessel was spun around like a toy, careening bow first down the face of the wave. When it hit the trough, the bow buried itself in the water and the stern was lifted up and over the bow, "pitch-poling" the boat. Ernie Hazard and the three other crewmen were upside down in the flooded wheelhouse struggling to find a way out.

Only Ernie escaped the sinking boat. He found a small air pocket, grabbed a bite of air, and then swam downward toward a small area of gray light. His head collided with an intact window, and finding no escape, Ernie decided to return to the air pocket, but it was gone. With his last seconds of breath, he dove down once more, groping in the darkness for an exit from the pilothouse. Locating a small opening, Ernie swam through it and kicked toward the surface, his lungs screaming for air.

Reaching the surface, Ernie encountered so much foam it was hard to breathe. He was on the windward side of the overturned vessel, and despite his efforts to stay with the boat, the wind and waves were pushing it much faster than he could swim. Kicking his boots off and squirming out of his jacket, he struggled for gulps of air in the foam.

Debris from the *Fair Wind* swirled around Ernie and with his strength ebbing he grabbed a bucket and turned it over, trapping air inside. This provided him with enough buoyancy to get his head above the foam. He could see the boat—his only real chance of survival—drifting farther away.

One would think that Ernie was out of options. Most of us likely would have held onto the bucket to keep from drowning, but in doing so sealed our fate. We might last another half hour but still be killed by the combination of pounding waves and the fifty-five-degree water. But Ernie, as I came to realize after interviewing him over multiple days, processed information quickly *despite* his fear. While the bucket was keeping him alive, he knew it wasn't the answer to his survival. "I had a decision to make. I could stay with the bucket that acted as a float when the seas weren't burying me. Or I could risk everything and let go of the bucket to try and get back to the boat by swimming and body surfing down the waves. It was an agonizing decision. I did not want to let go of that bucket." Yet somehow he did just that, knowing the overturned boat was the better option, really the only option, to long-term survival.

Ernie made it to the capsized *Fair Wind,* but the hull was too slippery to hold onto, so he swam around it to the vessel's other side. That's where he found the inflated life raft still tethered to the vessel!

The raft was approximately six feet across with a domed canopy above and a ballast bag hanging underneath for stability. Ernie heaved himself inside, hoping to find his crewmembers waiting for him, but the tiny vessel was empty.

Each time a wave pounded the *Fair Wind,* the life raft jerked violently and Ernie was afraid the tether would rip the raft's fabric. He wanted to untie the tether, but he thought maybe his buddies might still make it out of the vessel. So he decided to risk staying right where he was, sticking his head out of the raft from time to time to look for his friends.

After forty-five minutes Ernie saw that the hull of the boat was clearly sinking, so he quickly untied the tether from the raft. Now the seas, which seemed like a living, breathing beast out to destroy him, had complete control of the raft and sent it spinning and tumbling into the void. Ernie hung on inside, feeling like he was a punching bag, terrified he'd be thrown from the raft.

So far, Ernie had made two crucial decisions and done so correctly: the first was letting go of the bucket and the second was to untie the raft from the *Fair Wind* just before it sank. There would be more decisions, and I compare them to taking a test where your score has to be a perfect 100 percent to continue to live. But Ernie had something going for him that was crucial to his survival: throughout his fifty-hour ordeal he fully utilized the power of little steps. Those steps buoyed his spirits and motivated him to fight just a little bit longer. Equally important: he paused before implementing a decision, trying to think of all its ramifications and consequences.

In the first few minutes after the raft was freed from its tether, a wave slammed it so hard Ernie was thrown from his life-saving capsule. Fortunately, he was able to swim back to the raft and crawl in. Panting and shivering in five inches of water sloshing around the floor he considered lashing himself inside to prevent being tossed out again. But Ernie ultimately rejected the idea, afraid that if the raft did a 180-degree roll, he'd be firmly secured upside down and drown.

Just a few minutes later, that's exactly what happened, and Ernie found himself struggling underwater to kick free of the upside-down raft. Once outside he hung on to the ballast bag, but the waves kept collapsing on him, making it difficult to maintain his grasp. Minutes went by and again he made a small step—but a big decision—that likely saved his life. He climbed inside the ballast bag, curling up in the fetal position. This allowed him some protection from the 100 mile per hour winds and, just as important, it kept him in full contact with the raft so it wouldn't blow away. His ingenuity allowed him to live a bit longer, and he told himself, *fight you son of a bitch, hang in there.*

Later a wave knocked the raft right-side up and Ernie had to swim out of the submerged ballast bag and scramble into the raft before it blew away. He experimented with different sitting positions to keep the raft from tumbling, and even tried lying down in the water that collected on the vessel's floor.

Throughout Ernie's ordeal he kept despair at bay by talking to himself, giving himself pats on the back when he made the right move or the correct decision, saying, *good job, Ernie, now keep it going.* But every now and then he couldn't help but think what a long shot it would be for the Coast Guard to come...if they came. The rogue wave had hit so suddenly Captain Billy Garnos never had a chance to radio a Mayday. *Don't think of it. Just get through the next hour,* Ernie counseled himself.

And like Brad Cavanaugh, that's what he did. He tackled one hour at a time, focusing on the *now* and the few things he could control. When I asked Ernie if he was worried about sharks, he laughed, and said, "Mike, sharks were the least of my worries. Drowning or hypothermia was going to kill me." Brad Cavanaugh had a similar response to the same question and said, "Even though there were sharks all around the raft, I tried not to pay them any attention. They were out of my control. I was focused on what I could do next to make our situation better."

The psychological boost of ignoring what's out of your control and experimenting with what's within your control cannot be overstated. We are all guilty of worrying about the wrong things. On a personal note, Brad and Ernie taught me to be smarter about which problems I should work on while letting go of issues beyond my control.

I realized I'd been using the power of little steps in my writing life to overcome the feeling of being overwhelmed. So many times I've heard aspiring authors say they have a great book idea but felt so beleaguered they gave up. My answer? Break that big goal of a book down to little steps. Start by just thinking about one chapter, don't look beyond that. Have a file for that chapter or sub-files as well. Then when you complete the chapter, give yourself some positive reinforcement. Talk to yourself, tell yourself you did a good job, just like Ernie did.

Ernie's survival was beyond all reasonable expectation. In fact, on Coast Guard survivability charts for hypothermia, Ernie should have died within the first half of his ordeal. He is living proof the mind can prod the body forward. I interviewed the Coast Guardsman who was on the cutter that found Ernie and who then put out in a launch to go to the life raft. Tom McKenzie told me he expected the life raft to be either empty or have dead crewmen inside. When his launch was just a couple feet from the raft, the doorway of the raft parted. A head appeared, and McKenzie told me: "I'll never forget that moment because his [Ernie's] skin was blue. His bare chest was blue, his arms were blue, and his face and neck were blue. Then beneath this big bushy beard I saw this man smile. I simply could not believe he could smile after what he must have endured."

So next time you have a goal that seems insurmountable, block out the naysayers, keep making those little steps and be like Ernie who proved that hypothermia charts aren't always right. They can't measure the added benefits of pure determination.

## SURVIVOR LESSONS FOR YOUR LIFE:

- When you are in a jam, say to yourself "how can I improve this situation."

- Ernie and Brad focused on the few things in their control and did their best to block out despair that can lead to resignation. To sear this lesson into your memory, recall how I asked Ernie if he was afraid of sharks, and his answer was "Mike, sharks were the least of my worries." Brad's answer to the same question: "Sharks were out of my control. I was focused on what I could do next to make our situation better."

- If you think there is no aspect of your situation that is in your control, think again. You always have control over one factor: your reaction.

- Continually making little steps toward your goal will get you there. It will likely take time, with many twists and turns, so be sure to celebrate each achievement on the journey.

- Repeating a positive, encouraging statement helped Brad survive: "Don't give up. Our luck is bound to change." You might consider crafting your own positive statement and repeat it often. Whether you are facing a serious problem or going after a difficult goal, repeating that statement helps keep you on track, focused, and hopeful.

- Fear is natural and should not be avoided. Courage is continuing to act despite the fear.

- So many of us get overwhelmed when faced with a difficult challenge. But we can respond like Brad and Ernie: focus on one hour at a time and keep making those little steps.

## CHAPTER 2

# THINKING OUTSIDE ONESELF

*"I'm going to bring Tom home."*

—Loch Reidy

## THE DESIRE TO BEAR WITNESS

The will to live is strengthened by having a reason bigger than oneself to endure. In many survival stories, the survivor has a driving mission to tell the world what happened. Time and time again, survivors of concentration camps and gulags, and those held captive, cite the need to bear witness, to tell others of the horrors inflicted upon them as the reason they persisted. Elie Wiesel, a Nobel laureate and concentration camp survivor, said it best: "The victims elect to become witnesses."

In his book *The Holocaust Kingdom*, Alexander Donat describes the daily suffering in the Warsaw Ghetto at the hands of the Nazis. His resolution was to survive so that he could tell others what happened and never be silenced. "I felt I was a witness to disaster and charged with the sacred mission of carrying the Ghetto's history through the flames and barbed wire until such time as I could hurl it into the face of the world. It seemed to me that this sense of mission gave me the strength to endure everything." And endure he did, through both the Ghetto uprising and the concentration camps of Auschwitz and Dachau. The need to record what happened was indeed a mission, a mission to hold those accountable for their crimes, but also to warn future generations that evil is ever-present and must be crushed when it first rears its head. This passion to testify to the atrocities gives the survivor a purpose much bigger than his own life. The fewer survive, the more urgent is the purpose that the truth come out.

For Viktor Frankl, who survived the Holocaust, the need to tell the world what happened gave him a reason to "look to the future." He tried to imagine upcoming years as happy and productive, visualizing himself on stage, telling the public about the terrors in the concentration camps. He knew that "the prisoner who lost faith in the future—his future—was doomed."

Frankl used his imagination to see himself in the future explaining what he, and those who did not make it, had endured. The Nazis' reign of cruelty could take everything from a man or woman and reduce them to unspeakable deprivation, but the captors could not take Frankl's imagination and sense of purpose. He survived four Nazi death camps, and later used his freedom to describe what happened and how he survived in several books. What he imagined ultimately came true.

Revenge coupled with the need to have the truth be told is also a strong motivator when a person's suffering is caused by another. When sailors on the *Bounty* mutinied on April 28, 1789, Captain Bligh and eighteen loyal men were set adrift on an open launch— just twenty-three feet long—with minimal provisions. Indeed, the supply of food and water was expected to last a mere five days.

Incredibly, Bligh and his men traveled over 3,500 miles in the course of forty-eight days and reached safety—an unbelievable act of seamanship. Bligh kept a journal on the little vessel and later expanded it into book form. He wrote of how he conceived to survive "so heavy a calamity, to be able to account to my King and Country for my misfortune." One of Bligh's best decisions during this odyssey occurred shortly after he was set adrift. Bligh and his loyal followers landed on the island of Tofua, where they rejoiced, finding fresh water and coconuts. Perhaps this island could be a base from which to either live until discovered by another ship, or stay long enough to provision their launch with food and water for many days at sea.

Tofua, however, was not an uninhabited island, and after spending three days there, Bligh was approached by local natives. The captain began trading buttons and beads for food, and all seemed well. But more natives appeared each hour, crowding around the intruders. After a couple of days of bartering with the natives, Bligh wrote "I observed some symptoms of a design against us." Sensing trouble, Bligh ordered his men to stand by the launch while he finished trading with the islanders. When Bligh heard the natives clacking stones, he knew from his experience on Cook's third voyage to the Pacific (where Cook was killed) that an attack was imminent, and he made his way to the launch. All the men piled in except John Norton, who was on shore to cast off the stern line. Norton was immediately killed by the mob, and Bligh and his men pulled away in the launch. Canoes filled with angry natives chased after the Englishmen, and Bligh instructed his men to throw clothing overboard in the hopes the villagers would stop paddling to gather it. The plan worked, and the sailors escaped.

The castaways then had to make a difficult decision: Should they stop at other islands they might come across, or skip the islands and try to make it to Timor, which Bligh correctly estimated was over 3,500 miles away? The men, with Bligh leading the discussion, felt their chances were better at sea than risking ambush on an island by hostile natives. Imagine how difficult that choice was, knowing the islands held food and water, but might also bring instant death. They opted to ignore what I refer to as the illusion of comfort that the islands offered and instead trusted in their seamanship and Bligh's leadership to do the near-impossible.

When a storm exploded and pummeled their vessel with rampaging seas, the sailors had to lighten the boat, and they discarded extra sails, clothes, and anything else not deemed absolutely essential. Food was rationed, and as their hardtack dwindled, each man was only allowed a mere bite, twice daily, with a bit of salt pork and four ounces of water. Bligh did his best to add some routine and structure through the painful days by encouraging storytelling, singing, and fixed times to carefully measure out the food for each man. The men knew the odds of survival were bleak at best, but they never turned on one another, even when some began to give up hope. But more than forty-eight days after the *Bounty* mutiny, having suffered every deprivation imaginable, they made it to Timor. Bligh did indeed tell the world what happened, and got a measure of revenge against some of the men who had mutinied.

As remarkable as Bligh's feat was, the saga of mountain man Hugh Glass's survival story might be even more astonishing because Glass achieved his goal alone. Glass was attacked by a grizzly bear in 1823, when he was with a fur trading and trapping party in South Dakota. His comrades, upon seeing Glass lying on the ground with gaping wounds in a pool of blood, assumed him dead, but on closer examination, they could hear his labored breathing. Two of his party later recalled he had been "tore nearly all to pieces" and that Glass had "not less than fifteen wounds, any one of which under ordinary circumstances would have been considered mortal." They put Glass on a litter and continued their mission, expecting him to die within the day. But two days later he was still alive, and carrying him was slowing the party's progress. Two men were assigned to stay with Glass until he died, bury him, and then rejoin the party.

But again, Glass refused to die. The two healthy men feared being discovered by Native Americans (while also still under the impression that Glass was a goner), so they decided to move on without Glass. And why leave a perfectly good hunting rifle and knife with a dead man? They took those with them, and when they rejoined the rest of the party they lied, saying Glass had expired and they had buried him.

Glass rallied, however, and despite being without supplies and having wounds to the throat, legs, and elsewhere, started crawling south. His objective was not just to survive, but to seek revenge against the two men who had left him, and to regain his favorite rifle. Like the survivors of the concentration camps, he wanted the truth to be known about what had really happened to him. That burning desire fueled him as he crawled, and later limped, toward Fort Kiowa, South Dakota, 300 miles away! He was assisted in the last one hundred miles by friendly Native Americans. This was one tenacious man, and it's a shame Glass himself did not write down exactly how he pulled off this feat. But the story is told by those who were with him during the bear attack, those at the Fort when he stumbled in, and later by other mountain men who had conversations with him. It's a fragmented story at best, but once again shows that surviving to bear witness is strong motivation indeed. [The movie *The Revenant* is a fictionalized version of Glass's ordeal, which captures the essence of his fighting spirit.]

## THINKING OF OTHERS

Although revenge and bearing witness are strong motivators, the need to live for family seems to be the most frequent driving force that helps survivors carry on when they feel like giving up. Infantry radio operator Tom Coakley, featured in the book *Boom* and on NPR, credits this kind of thinking for saving his life in Vietnam. It was 1969, and Coakley and his company were thirty miles outside Saigon when they spotted North Vietnamese troops and advanced to engage the enemy. Coakley was ordered to extend his long whip radio antenna upward. This was not the kind of command he welcomed—he knew it would make him an easy target with the antenna sticking up skyward over the brush. He had never done this in the field before, but he couldn't even argue, because the orders were coming from a colonel in a helicopter hovering high above. Coakley had his orders and did as he was told.

His company advanced, not knowing there was a hidden North Vietnamese bunker directly in front of them. Minutes later a grenade landed just a foot in front of Coakley. It exploded, blowing the young soldier into the air, shattering one arm, almost severing one leg, and shredding the other. When a medic reached him, Coakley could feel the life force draining out of him and knew he would soon be dead.

Out of nowhere, he thought of his family back home and it hit him; *I can't die over here and leave them like this.* "I will always believe that this focus on something other than me in the terror of the moment is what saved my life," Coakley recalled.

Interestingly, the drive to bear witness and thoughts of family combine to make a strong driving force, even if the survivor expects to die shortly after rescue. In a tragic boat accident involving Nick Schuyler, Will Bleakley, and NFL players Corey Smith and Marquis Cooper, only Schuyler survived. They were fishing in the Gulf of Mexico when their anchor got stuck on the bottom. In an effort to free the anchor, they made the mistake of tying the anchor line to the stern of their boat and then gunning the engine, figuring either the anchor would come up or the rope would break. Instead, the boat capsized within two seconds. The men hung onto the overturned vessel, but with the water temperature at sixty-four degrees and air temperature dropping into the low forties, hypothermia began picking off the men one by one during their forty-four-hour ordeal in the water.

Schuyler, watching his friends die and feeling total despair and helplessness, later wrote, "I knew I needed to get through this to explain to them [the families] what happened. I needed to live long enough to tell the story, even if I was found alive and died later. If I didn't make it, people would tell their own stories based on rumors." He also thought of his mother, and used her as additional fuel not to give up. Schuyler fought to stay alive to spare her the pain his death would cause, later telling her, "I wasn't going to let you go to my funeral. I knew it would kill you."

Nick was still thinking of others when he decided to tell his story to the public. He wanted to help boaters avoid making some of the mistakes he and his buddies had. One of the lessons I learned from his book is that, when I'm fishing out on the ocean, I need to always leave a "float plan" with someone onshore, letting them know where I plan to fish and what time I expect to return home. And I learned the dangers of trying to free a stuck anchor.

Captain Tom Tighe, age sixty-five, from Patterson, NY, had made the voyage between Connecticut and Bermuda forty-eight times, and his first mate, fifty-seven-year-old Lochlin Reidy, had joined him on twenty of those trips. In early May of 2005, the two sailors embarked on yet another Bermuda-bound cruise, this time taking along three new crewmembers who wished to learn more about offshore sailing. The new crew included Kathy Gilchrist, Ron Burd, and Chris Ferrer.

The trouble started on the fourth day of the trip, when a storm-generated rogue wave came roaring down on the sailboat, the *Almeisan*. Kathy, Tom, and Loch were in the cockpit when they heard an oncoming roar like the engines of a jet. Then they felt the deck fall out from beneath them and were airborne before being pushed underwater. All three were smothered in seething white water, as if being hurled down a waterfall. Kathy was swept completely out of the boat and felt the ocean tugging, trying to separate her from the lifeline of her safety harness. She kicked to the surface and screamed.

Loch and Tom were pinned in the overturned cockpit, underwater. When the boat righted itself, they heard shouts for help. They knew it was Kathy, but in the darkness it took them a few seconds to realize she was outside the boat. They located her in the water and grabbed her safety harness, but the men didn't have the strength to pull her on board.

Below, Ron Burd had been thrown into the deck head, nearly knocking him unconscious. Chris, who had been resting in the galley beneath two windows, had narrowly escaped death when one of the windows shattered and torrents of glass and water rained down on him. Chris heard the shouting from above and scrambled topside, and along with Loch and Tom managed to pull Kathy back into the boat.

Tom inspected the battered condition of the vessel and the rising water inside, and made the fateful decision to activate the EPIRB [emergency beacon] and abandon ship via the life raft.

In the next few minutes, things went horribly wrong. As the crew assembled in the exposed cockpit, Tom inflated the life raft, but the wind blew it out twenty-five feet from the boat to the end of its tether. The tether was thin, and Tom handed the line to Loch while he scrambled to get gloves for a better grip and to prevent the line from cutting their hands. Returning with the gloves, the men were able to pull the raft to within five feet of the boat, but they could not bring it any closer. Loch, fearing the thin tether would break, knew they needed a heavier line secured to the raft to bring it next to the boat, where they could safely board. Wasting no time, he unclipped his safety harness tether from the boat's lifeline and dove from the boat through the open doorway of the domed life raft. Now inside the raft, he shouted for Ron to throw him a heavier line.

Just then, another rogue wave, perhaps fifty feet in size, slammed into the *Almeisan* and the life raft. The raft broke from its tether, did a complete 360, and hurled Loch into the sea. Tom and Ron were thrown from the boat, and Tom's harness snapped free from the safety line. He and Loch were engulfed by the breaking seas, but they swam to each other and clipped their safety harnesses together as the waves swept them far from the boat and into the void.

Onboard the *Almeisan*, Ron was outside the vessel, but hanging onto the rail that encircled the boat. Kathy and Chris pulled him aboard, dragging him into the cockpit. When Ron regained his senses he asked, "Where are Tom and Loch?" Chris shook his head, "Overboard. They're both gone."

With no life raft, the three sailors on the damaged *Almeisan* needed to keep the boat afloat until help arrived. They were in for the fight of their lives. But for the purposes of this story, we follow Tom and Loch, alone in the storm-tossed seas, 300 miles from land.

The two sailors were continually buried by avalanching waves, but in the troughs of the waves the men were able to talk of rescue, survival strategies, and their families, knowing the odds of escaping from their predicament alive were slim. As each hour passed, the men weakened, especially Tom, the older of the two. He didn't think he'd survive the constant beating and swallowing of seawater each time a wave drove him down.

Tom tried to give his life vest to Loch, but Loch shouted encouragement, and refused the vest. "No way!" shouted Loch, "I need you with me. I promise I'll get you home." He reminded Tom that the EPIRB was activated and the Coast Guard would be searching. But Loch also noticed Tom was clutching his chest, and he wondered if his friend had suffered a heart attack.

Soon, Tom's head was sagging, and Loch positioned him so he didn't' take the waves directly in the face. After ten hours of constantly fighting the seas, Tom stopped breathing in Loch's arms. Loch gave him mouth-to-mouth resuscitation, but Tom expired.

What Loch did next was out of love for his friend, but the action might also have helped saved Loch's life. With tears flowing, Loch thought about the way Tom tried to give him his life vest, reflecting how Tom had never complained, right up to his last breath. Loch decided he would not let Tom go, and he kept Tom's safety harness clipped to his own. He made a silent vow to bring his friend's body home.

There wasn't much Loch could do to increase his odds of survival, but he started preparing his mind for the long haul. He was dehydrated, hypothermic, and exhausted, and there wasn't anything he could do about it. Instead, he focused on his emotions, knowing that his feeling of helplessness was as big an enemy as the sea. To counteract the emotional low, he talked to himself about what he could do. *I'm going to bring Tom home, and I'm going to hang on for however long it takes because the Coast Guard will come.* He repeated *the Coast Guard will come—be ready* each time a particularly vicious wave drove him so far below the surface of the ocean his ears popped.

Somehow, he made it through the day and, with dusk falling, he steeled himself for the terror of spending an entire night alone in the dark seas. He had a strobe light, and he had seen and heard a Coast Guard C-130 aircraft searching for him. Holding the strobe light atop his head, he wondered if such a tiny light could be seen by those in the plane. He knew the pilot and crew had not seen him because the plane had gone directly over him, but it kept going without turning back. Loch sunk to the depths of despair. His energy was ebbing, and he thought the plane had left to search a new area.

His mission to bring Tom's body home gave him purpose, but he desperately needed warmth, water, and rest. The sea was wearing him down, and Loch could feel the creeping fingers of resignation taking hold of him, frightening him to the core. To shake himself from its grip, he thought of all the people he loved. Of those people, one person stood out: his thirteen-year-old daughter, Ashley. She was the one who needed him the most. And so Ashley became yet another reason to try and hang on a little longer. *I've got to live for Ashley.* Loch gave himself a pep talk, saying that he would battle until he was rescued so that he could be a part of his daughter's life.

Without fixing his mind first on bringing Tom's body home and later on his fight for Ashley, it is likely Loch would have closed his eyes and let the waves take away his pain. But with these additional reasons to battle on, he made it past midnight, outlasting hallucinations, teeth-chattering cold, and an exhaustion that seemed all-encompassing.

At 3:00 a.m., the storm still raged. Loch had been in the water twenty-four hours and knew the end was near. He fought to stay awake, and was rewarded when the C-130 came out of the clouds. Loch waved his miniscule strobe light, but the plane flew on.

Loch didn't know it, but one of the crew members in the plane had seen him, and they in turn instructed an oil tanker to proceed in his direction. The oil tanker arrived near Loch's position, but finding him at night was a long shot. Loch's strobe was failing, its light so dim that the men on the tanker could not see the lone survivor lashed to his captain's body in the storm-tossed seas.

Giving weak shouts, Loch hoped the men on the tanker could hear him over the waves, but the ship's searchlight scanned everywhere except on Loch. Soon the searchlight was extinguished. Loch thought the ship was going to leave, and with his last bit of strength decided to swim *around* the enormous tanker in hopes that one pair of eyes or ears could home in on him.

Imagine the frustration and fear that Loch felt, being so close to salvation and thinking the ship might leave at any moment. He pushed Tom's body ahead of him, and when he'd completely circled the ship, he realized no one had seen him. "Help!" he cried, with every ounce of energy he had.

That one shout was heard by the crew, and Loch was saved.

But what led up to the one last cry for help? It was Loch's mindset that he had to live for others. In his lowest moments, when Loch was ready to let the seas take him, he found strength in fighting just a little bit longer for Tom and Ashley.

As I wrote this chapter, I began reading about dory man Howard Blackburn, and couldn't help but notice how certain aspects of his ordeal and mindset were eerily similar to Lochlin Reidy's. Blackburn's story occurred in 1883 and Loch's was in 2005, but despite the years between them, the lessons are as apt today as ever.

Howard Blackburn, from Gloucester, Massachusetts, had signed on with the fishing schooner *Grace L. Fears*, bound for the waters off Newfoundland. He and a fellow fisherman, Thomas Welch, were in a dory hauling nets, not far from the mother ship, when a blinding snowstorm slammed into their little vessel, preventing them from reaching the *Grace L. Fears*. To make matters worse, night closed in. They first dropped anchor, but they realized the waves would be too much for the dory and instead fashioned a sea anchor that would drag behind the boat to slow their drift. Waves still spilled into the boat, and the men bailed as fast as they could. Blackburn lost his mittens in the process, and soon his hands began to freeze.

The men took turns bailing throughout the night and the next day, but the *Fears* could not find them. Welch died from exposure that night, so Howard moved his body and laid him down in the stern.

Blackburn's hands were now frozen solid, but somehow he got them around the oars and started rowing for shore, which he estimated was forty miles away. "The friction of the oar handles soon wore away the frozen flesh on my hands," he later explained. Yet he still continued to row, and before nightfall on the fourth day, he reached land.

Unfortunately, he landed in a remote part of Newfoundland. He was able to row up the mouth of a river and locate a fisherman's hut but found it abandoned. Unable to sleep, and perhaps worried about freezing to death if he did, he spent the night in the hut walking back and forth. In the morning he realized he'd have to get back in the dory and continue rowing until he found help.

The dory had filled with water during the night, but Welch's body was still in it. Blackburn tried to haul him up on a broken wharf, but the fisherman's body slipped and fell into the water.

Somehow Blackburn emptied and repaired the dory as best he could and started rowing. Later that day, he was spotted by a villager. "Soon every man and woman in the neighborhood came out on the ice to see who I was and what I wanted. When they saw my hands they cried, 'Your poor hands, go to the house at once.'"

Incredibly, Blackburn's thoughts were not just focused on himself, but also on his dead friend Welch. "I answered, 'I cannot just now, I want a couple of men to get in the dory with me and go down the mouth of the river for my dory-mate.'"

Lochlin Reidy, when he was finally rescued, had similar words to his rescuers. The men on the oil tanker lowered a cargo net to Loch, who was bobbing in the ocean, totally spent from his ordeal. Loch first put Tom's body in the net, and then he crawled in. While the net was being lifted, Tom's body fell out, back into the ocean.

When the rescuers laid Loch out on the ship's deck, the captain of the oil tanker said, "You kept your captain with you all this time?" Loch croaked, "Yes. He's dead, but you have to get him."

"We will, we will," answered the ship's captain—just like the villagers on Newfoundland did when they told Blackburn they would recover Tom Welch's body.

One incredible component to Blackburn's story is what he did after his ordeal. He didn't just survive, he thrived, which I've observed with so many of the survivors I've gotten to know. Despite losing the fingers on both hands as well as his toes, Blackburn did not let that stop him from pursuing his dreams. He became a successful businessman in Gloucester, Massachusetts, and then surprised the entire town by announcing that he planned to sail across the Atlantic, alone! A man with no fingers facing the very ocean that had taken them from him.

In 1899, Blackburn set out in a thirty-foot sloop that he christened *Great Western*. He faced illness, stormy weather that produced a waterspout, and almost being run down by the bow of a giant steamer, but he made it safely to England in sixty-two days. At that time, he became only the sixth person to complete the solo crossing, and certainly the first to do it without the aid of his fingers. Then two years later he did it again, in an even smaller vessel of just twenty-five feet, in thirty-nine days! That was a record crossing that stood for many years.

Imagine the courage, ingenuity, and determination it took to face the ocean again voluntarily. In many respects, Blackburn's successful "second act" after his survival-at-sea saga is similar to many of the survivors I've interviewed over the years. While some may suffer from post-traumatic stress syndrome, most not only make a full recovery but move forward with their lives, not letting the harrowing event they experienced define them or stop them from seeking adventure. And later in this book you will see the way their experiences changed them, often in surprising ways.

It behooves the rest of us to pay attention to the ways these survivors' lives were enriched after their survival. We can emulate them to a certain degree without having to suffer a life-or-death experience. In fact, my personal mantra has been, "I'd be a fool not to incorporate some of the changes they made into my own life." These survivors have looked into the abyss, risen to their various challenges, and decided to improve their lives as a result.

The various incidents described in this chapter are only the tip of the iceberg when it comes to the sheer number of survivors who later said what kept them going was their family, their buddies in combat, or a friend who had died. An example that encompasses the essence of this mindset is the observations of Lewis Haynes, who was the doctor aboard the *USS Indianapolis* when it was sunk during WWII. He experienced the horrors of watching many young men die from shark attack, exposure, exhaustion, or drinking seawater. During his days adrift at sea, Dr. Haynes couldn't help but notice which of the young sailors were the most determined to survive. Doug Stanton, author of *In Harm's Way*, describes a scene where the doctor is doing his best to keep the young sailors in his group alive and determined. "Some of the boys now asked him [Haynes] if they could evaporate the salt from the seawater by cupping it in their hands and holding it up to the sun. He gently shook his head, told them, "No, son," and begged the boys to be patient. He began keeping a close eye on those he knew weren't married or were without close ties on shore. Those with families, he discovered, were fighting the temptation to drink from the sea."

Dr. Haynes was neither the first nor the last to observe this pattern; it has also been documented with life-altering diseases. Caryle Hirshberg, in *Remarkable Recovery*, interviewed long-term survivors and found that those who were connected to a life partner or a community did far better than those who were in relative social isolation.

Thinking of others is not just for dire situations. It can give all of us a rock to hold onto and a sense of purpose larger than ourselves during the bumps in life's road. So expand your group of friends and loved ones—it might just save your life.

# SURVIVOR LESSONS FOR YOUR LIFE:

- When you feel like giving up, an additional incentive to fight on can be found by thinking of loved ones, especially someone who might depend on you.

- Loch used a "mantra," *the Coast Guard is coming*, combining that with his own part in his rescue in the form of *be ready*. We can use that same kind of combination when it seems an objective is slipping out of reach.

- If you are the victim of injustice, you can gain strength by holding the goal of telling others what really happened. Your revenge might be the satisfaction of a court of law righting the wrong or imparting true justice.

- During difficult times, add structure to your day. Even when you don't feel like getting out of bed, force yourself to go through a routine. That small bit of structure helps the time pass, and often allows you to regroup and achieve your goal.

CHAPTER 3

# CONTROL, REACTION, DETACH

"I was able to fill my mind with the fine and comforting things of the world. I surrounded myself with my family and my friends. I projected myself into the sunlight, into the midst of green, growing things."

—Admiral Richard E. Byrd

Admiral Richard E. Byrd had won acclaim as the first man to fly over the North Pole (disputed) and for leading several expeditions to the South Pole. In the winter of 1934, he decided to set up a weather station in interior Antarctica and live there—in a tiny hut—for five months alone, something no one had ever done before. Talk about self-isolating!

Byrd viewed the mission as both a challenge and a period of solitude he would embrace. "I should be able to live exactly as I chose, obedient to no necessities but those imposed by the wind and night and cold, and to no man's laws but my own. Perhaps the desire was also in my mind to try a more rigorous existence than any I had known." He got all that, and much more.

The Admiral almost died of carbon monoxide poisoning in his little hut because of a faulty stove pipe. Seriously ill, he had to find a way to survive until rescue could come with the spring thaw. At first, he wasn't aware his symptoms were caused by carbon monoxide, but even when he discovered the cause of his illness, he still needed to use the stove periodically to keep from freezing to death. "The fire was my enemy," Byrd wrote, "but I could not live without it."

There may not be a more desolate, depressing place on Earth to be battling sickness alone. The Antarctic winter has no sunlight, and Byrd was largely confined to his gloomy, snow-covered hut, which became so cold that ice froze on the inside walls. Outside, sub-zero temperatures were the norm. Byrd kept notes during his struggle and later wrote a book about his experience, *Alone*, which explains how he managed to keep his sanity and stay alive.

Some of his biggest battles had to do with sensory deprivation, lack of distractions, and loneliness. It seemed sheer boredom could drive a man mad. His answer was to have a routine of simple tasks, or else "the days would have been without purpose: and without purpose they would have ended, as such days always had, in disintegration." Prior to the carbon monoxide poisoning, he helped break the monotony by digging himself out of his snowbound cave and taking a short walk. But with the illness, his strength was sapped, and he was confined inside his icy tomb.

In the beginning of his poisoning, he was certain he would die: "Life seldom ends gracefully or sensibly. The protesting body succumbs like a sinking ship." He went on to describe how even getting water was almost beyond his power. "My thirst was the tallest tree in a forest of pain. The escape tunnel was [seemingly] a hundred miles away, but I started out, carrying the bucket and lantern. Somewhere along the way I slipped and fell. I licked the snow until my tongue burned." He then switched tactics and went to his nearby food tunnel, where he found that he could scrape dirty snow into his bucket and then pull it to the shack "a foot or so at a time."

That line jumps out as both a literal and figurative illustration of the power of little steps. But Byrd needed much more than those steps, because of the isolation. He had to fill time in a productive way, and there wasn't much within his control. Recognizing that the days stretched out endlessly before him until a possible spring rescue, he fought the urge to just lie in his sleeping bag for warmth.

"Nevertheless, I was able to do a number of small things, in a series of stealthy, deliberate sorties from the bunk. I attended to the inside thermograph and register, changing the sheets, winding the clocks, and inking the pen." Any activity he had the strength to perform gave him a moment's reprieve from the overwhelming melancholy.

Like other survivors, he wanted to live for his family, and felt guilt for the pain they would suffer if he didn't make it out alive. After all, his ordeal/experiment was voluntary. His illness and isolation crystallized how central his family was to his happiness, well-being, and sense of reason for living. "Great waves of fear, a fear I had never known before, swept through me and settled deep within. But it wasn't the fear of suffering or even of death itself. It was a terrible anxiety over the consequence of those at home if I failed to return. I saw my whole life pass in review. I realized how wrong my sense of values had been and how I had failed to see that the simple, homely, unpretentious things of life are the most important."

Byrd berated himself for making this risky venture, but without the experience, would he have come to realize the importance of family? "At the end only two things really matter to a man, regardless of who he is: and they are the affection and understanding of his family. Anything and everything else he creates are insubstantial..."

Loch Reidy's thoughts of his daughter sustained his will to fight on, and Byrd had done something similar. But, in total isolation for many days, he was on the verge of giving up. "Up until now I had been sustained by a conviction that the only way I could nullify my mistake and make reparation to my family was by transcending myself and surviving. But I had lost. I flung my arms across the table and put my head down.... I felt no shame then, although I do now. Fear was gone, also. When hope goes, uncertainty goes, too; and men don't fear certainties."

From that lowest of low points, he gathered what little strength he had and wrote a message to his wife. His final outcome was not in his control, nor did he believe he would survive, but the simple act of putting his thoughts on paper had a positive effect. "The frenzy to write supplied its own strength. After the first few paragraphs my mind calmed."

The simple act of writing was a little step in his resurgence from rock bottom, and soon he was writing to his mother, his children, and colleagues. "Something approaching gratitude flowed into me." This was followed by thinking of his younger days at the Naval Academy, where he wrestled for the welterweight championship. He remembered how he given up all hope of winning but fought on so as not to shame his mother in the gallery. "The same determination that had kept me fighting on to the finish that day again came surging back. I saw that although I seemed absolutely washed up, there was a chance I was mistaken."

Reading Byrd's prose, you feel his loneliness and desperation, but you also see how he was trying to corral the one thing left in his control, which was his reaction to his plight. He could curl up in his sleeping bag and die, or he could see his task through to the end, no matter the outcome. Although he had briefly rallied by writing the letters, he soon fell right back into desperate despondency. And this time, he thought of another choice that must have looked quite appealing: a bottle of sleeping pills. "The sleeping pills were on the shelf. The flashlight fingered the bottle. I took it down and dumped the pellets into my cupped palm. They bespoke a lovely promise."

Byrd stopped himself from suicide, and instead started writing affirmations that he was not alone. "The universe is not dead. Therefore, there is an Intelligence there and it is all pervading... Though I am cut off from human beings, I am not alone." The mere act of writing those words was his salvation, and he repeated them over and over. He went back to doing the small chores in the hut. "I did what had to be done piecemeal, doling out my strength in miserly driblets, creeping rather than walking, resting long intervals after each small effort."

He had hit rock bottom, not once but twice, yet by taking control of both chores and his thoughts, he began to climb out of that "evil night." Byrd devised another technique to spur him onward: he directed his thoughts to pleasant memories. "I was able to fill my mind with the fine and comforting things of the world. I surrounded myself with my family and my friends. I projected myself into the sunlight, into the midst of green, growing things."

Byrd had difficulty staying in the world of imagination, but he kept at it, and that night had his best sleep since the start of the illness. In the morning he "was better in mind and body." The Admiral showed that, even on the edge of preferring death over life, he marshaled the one thing he could control—his thoughts—and turned them from despair to pleasant images that then reinforced his will to live. [Luck was with him also—at one point he was strong enough to briefly venture outside, only to have the hatch to his hut freeze solidly shut. Death would have come quickly had he not stumbled upon a shovel and used it to pry the hatch open.]

Somehow Byrd hung on for five months, trapped in the hut, before finally being rescued by a team of men from base camp at the coast. He had lost sixty pounds, but he was both alive and sane, in large part thanks to his focus on the few things he could control, especially his thoughts.

Earlier I described how Brad Cavanaugh, Ernie Hazard, and so many other incredible survivors tried to compartmentalize their thoughts. They illustrated the importance of ignoring, or at least spending minimal time on, what you cannot control, and instead focusing on the changes you can make.

In some survival situations—as well as in day-to-day life—the outlook or circumstance is so bleak it seems there is nothing in our control. But that is never the case, because the one thing we all have which can never be taken away is our *reaction*. Survivors have shown that only half the battle is physical; the other half is their response to what is happening around them and to them.

I'm particularly impressed by the actions of survivor Amy Racina, who fell sixty feet onto a granite ledge while hiking alone deep in the Sierra Nevada Mountains. The fall shattered her legs and hips, and she was unable to move either leg "so much as an inch." She had fallen from a remote path and, just as troublesome, she was not expected home for five or six more days, which meant no one would be searching for her until that time. In her book *Angels in the Wilderness* she wrote, "It's unacceptable to me to merely sit and wait. That would be like signing my death warrant. My best chance for survival is to get to a trail."

Amy knew it would be nearly impossible to drag her body uphill, so she decided to work with the terrain and crawl down the mountainside to a path where someone might find her. She realized, however, that the ravine trail had its own danger, because if it rained hard, she would be caught in a flash flood. Despite the agony of pain, her thoughts were lucid. She made up her mind that the ravine trail was her best hope, and that she simply could not dwell on the possibility of rain—something beyond her control. "Nothing I can do about that worry, so I put it aside."

Amy estimated the trail was almost a mile away—a seemingly insurmountable distance. But she combined two survival techniques: focus on what's in your control, and the power of taking little steps. "I am ready to go. I choose a goal that is ten yards away." In time, those goals of mere yards, led to salvation.

As bad as Amy's situation was, Aron Ralston's was worse. While hiking alone in the canyon lands of Southeast Utah, a massive boulder fell on his forearm, pinning him in place. Like Amy, Aron was in a remote region and knew that help would not be coming in the next few days. Early in his book *Between a Rock and a Hard Place*, he takes responsibility for his predicament, making the same mistake I've made several times when I was younger and in isolated mountain country. "I violated the prime directive of wilderness travel in failing to leave a detailed trip plan with a responsible person."

Aron was one tough individual, and he tried numerous ways to free his arm, such as using a small rock as a hammer to split or chip away at the large boulder. He recognized that taking action, even if futile, was keeping him from giving up. "Without even that minimal distraction, I have nothing whatsoever to do. I have no life. Only in action does my life approximate anything more than existence. Without any other task or stimulus, I'm no longer living, no longer surviving, I'm just waiting."

After days of trying to free himself with no progress, Aron was seemingly out of options. Or perhaps I should say, most of us would feel there was no solution, not one shred of control over the situation. Aron thought differently: he had one horrific option left, and that was to cut his own arm off. "Knowing the alternative is to wait for a progressively more certain but assuredly slow demise, I choose to meet the risk of death in action." There is much more to Aron's story, and his book offers a glimpse into his mindset, his honesty, and the many obstacles he had to overcome, including hiking and climbing several miles out of the canyons *after* severing his arm. Ralston is a remarkable soul, and like the other survivors I've discussed, has much to teach us far beyond the survival ordeal.

One beneficial reaction in a survival situation, or even in a non-life-threatening challenge, is to make up your mind to never stop fighting. That was the mindset of both Ernie Hazard and Brad

Cavanaugh, and it is right in sync with a more recent survivor, Jose Alvarenga, who, along with fellow fisherman Ezequiel Cordoba, was trapped aboard a twenty-three-foot skiff that lost engine power in a storm. This occurred off the coast of Mexico, and the boat then drifted for hundreds of miles across the Pacific. According to Alvarenga, about four months into their ordeal, Cordoba gave up hope after becoming sick from eating raw meat from birds they had caught. The suffering from exposure, dehydration, and lack of food was just too much for Cordoba, and he told Alvarenga that he thought he would be dead within the month. Alvarenga responded that they could hang on longer if they continued to catch and eat birds and turtles, and together they would show the world what they had overcome.

"I don't believe any of that," Cordoba answered. "We are going to die."

Alvarenga answered the same way Brad or Ernie would have: "Don't think about that. No one is going to die. You have to fight."

But Cordoba knew the odds were incredibly long. The fight had gone out of him, and he refused to eat the raw bird meat. He soon perished. Alvarenga, now alone, fought off overwhelming depression by imagining he was somewhere else, ranging from being in the arms of beautiful women to feasting at vast banquets offering every kind of food imaginable. He also forced his thoughts away from churning about the bleak odds of ultimate survival. Instead, the castaway focused on the little things in his control, such as catching birds and turtles, curling up inside a large cooler to escape the blazing sun, and taking other actions to prolong his life.

Alvarenga became a master at using his imaginary world to block out the deprivations of his real world on the boat. Author Jonathan Franklin wrote, in his book about this remarkable survivor, "Alvarenga imagined a reality so believable that he could later say with total honesty that alone at sea he tasted the greatest meals of his life and experienced the most delicious sex."

Alvarenga controlled the most important component in his hostile environment, his thoughts. He ultimately survived an astounding 438 days adrift before landing in the Marshall Islands.

The examples of survivors detaching from their bleak situations and escaping through imagination are numerous. Roy Hallums was an American contractor in Iraq who in 2004 was kidnapped, held captive, and beaten frequently for 311 days. Much of the time, he was held in a pitch-black pit. Few people could survive such conditions, either mentally or physically, but Hallums had several techniques within his control to ease his suffering. One was to transport himself away from the pit and take "mental road trips," where he traveled to places he had wanted to see. Using the power of imagination, he disengaged from his predicament and took a vacation, making a long, detailed journey from Arkansas through Texas, then onward into the Rocky Mountains.

Others held in captivity (or trapped like Byrd and Alvarenga) use similar detaching techniques to get through each day. Some have written songs, elaborate rhymes, and even entire novels, all in their heads, without the aid of pen and paper. American Sarah Shourd, held for almost fourteen months in an Iranian prison, said that the songs she composed while in confinement helped keep her soul alive. She found a purpose that both kept the creative part of her mind in use and relieved the boredom.

When I hear stories like Shourd's, I can't help but think of the working professionals who, upon retirement, lose their sense of purpose and become bored, living more for creature comforts rather than creating, producing, or problem-solving. I've yet to find a study that links these retirees' aimlessness to heart disease, but my hunch is that lack of purpose can kill, just as we know that inactivity kills.

Oscar Tulio Lizcano, held captive by Columbian rebels for eight years, created his detachment by conjuring imaginary students to lecture to. "At one point," Lizcano recounted after his escape, "I stuck sticks in the ground and put the names of people on them with notebook pages and we would 'study' for three hours a day."

Lizcano illustrated a tiny sliver of autonomy through the control of the one last bastion of freedom, his mind. His example is a lesson for all of us when we feel helpless: change our role (even if temporarily) from victim to survivor by taking the smallest of initiatives. That in turn fuels a bit of confidence and relief from the situation, simply because you took action. It reaffirms that your mind is your own, and you can use it to detach when you need a change of scenery, even if that scenery is in your head. In these cases of being trapped or in captivity, it's *the act of doing* that is helpful.

By exerting mental control, the survivors we have studied were coping as best they could with a terrible situation, buying themselves more time for ultimate rescue, salvation, or the lucky break they needed.

We have now seen the importance of using the imagination, positive affirmations, and a fighting spirit to outlast the darkest days. Equally important is self-talk, and in particular doing what I call celebrating the little steps achieved. Almost every survivor I've interviewed commented on this, whether the conversation was inside their head or spoken aloud during their ordeal. In a future chapter, we will explore the specifics of how the very best survivors—the ones who make it when 99 percent of us would probably succumb—use conversations with themselves to outlast their obstacles.

As I researched this chapter on control, reaction, and when to engage and when to detach, I was struck by the utility these techniques would offer for anyone depressed, stressed, or fighting an illness. I asked myself, *Why do certain people I know show few signs of stress in situations that would make most of us crumble?* After questioning these individuals, two answers, expressed in various ways, bubbled to the surface: they were doing "their best" and always sought out areas in the situation where they could take action, which in turn displayed a measure of control. Their responses were very similar to the techniques survivors described to me that helped them overcome their ordeals.

We talk ourselves into getting stressed by thinking we have absolutely no control. Fortunately, we can do the opposite: talk ourselves into a more calm and balanced approach by saying "I'm doing what I can to slowly change this situation." This declaration acknowledges some measure of influence to overcome the circumstances.

Whether it be an extreme survivor, like Richard Byrd, or someone successfully coping with an illness, the common technique was searching out even the tiniest action that showed control. The more they believed they could influence the outcome, rather than external forces having total control over their fate, the more they thought like a survivor rather than victim. We can do the same in our day-to-day life: search out the aspects of a bad situation where we can make a few moves, little steps, or incremental decisions that result in feelings of empowerment.

Whenever I start feeling like a victim, I catch myself, and instead say to myself, *I'm partly responsible for the situation in some small way, and I have the means to improve it—it is just going to take time.* This is a struggle for me because I'm an inherently impatient person, but time and time again, if I hold onto the image of the outcome I desire—and don't put a deadline on it—the bad situation gets resolved or my goal/dream is fulfilled. Working with survivors has only strengthened this conviction that the answer will come. I refuse to live life passively.

Contributing to depression and stress is the feeling that we are helpless in what is happening around us and to us. Medical professionals extend this notion to contributing to physical illnesses as well. One of my favorite books on this subject is *How Not to be My Patient*, by Edward Creagan, MD. He explains the attitudes and behaviors that patients can adopt to improve their health and recover more quickly from illness. Almost all the qualities he describes are the very ones that extreme survivors intuitively knew were the key to their beating the odds.

Central to Dr. Creagan's message and studies was that the patients who focused on what they could control rather than what they could not did the best. In his book, he expanded this fact to the measure of control we have in our jobs. Citing a study by a research team at the University of Texas led by Benjamin Amick III, PhD, it was found that workers with little opportunity for decision-making "die earlier than those with more flexibility, even if those flexible jobs are also in high-stress positions." The findings were quite conclusive: "workers with little control in their jobs were 43–50 percent more likely to die during a period of five to ten years than workers who had high-stress jobs but more decision-making responsibilities."

It is clear that surviving life-or-death events and staying healthy in your job both benefit from exercising some form of control.

The survivors I've worked with have given me so much to emulate, and two of the most important techniques I try to follow are: 1] I'm not going to worry about the little stuff or what's out of my control and instead focus on what I can influence, and 2] I believe that I can turn every "bad" situation into an experience I can learn from, and in most cases I can ultimately glean something positive from it. See if you can do the same.

Sometimes it's as easy as looking at the situation from a new perspective and announcing to yourself that your situation is not necessarily a bad thing in the long run. Then, using positive reaffirmation, believe that you are going to learn from the experience and later turn it into an asset or a life lesson that pays dividends each time a similar "problem" comes along.

## SURVIVOR LESSONS FOR YOUR LIFE:

- Richard Byrd teaches us that forcing ourselves to do small chores can get us through the darkest moments. Those chores give us a sense of purpose and usefulness until we can tackle bigger demands.

- Byrd uncovered two simple truths when he was alone and near death that are important reminders for all of us. *I realized how wrong my sense of values had been and how I had failed to see that the simple, homely, unpretentious things of life are the most important. At the end only two things really matter to a man, regardless of who he is: and they are the affection and understanding of his family.*

- When it seems not a single aspect of your situation is in your control, remember you always can exert influence on the most important component of your ordeal, your *reaction.*

- You have, and no one else has, command of your thoughts. When you need a break from a tough jam, temporarily detach and take flight to pleasant memories. Or, using the power of imagination, briefly disengage from your predicament and take a mental road trip. Those peaceful places you think about will come into your life again; you just have to let time pass, knowing better days are ahead.

- Think of every "bad" situation as an experience you can learn from. This will eventually help you develop the attitude that you can turn almost every situation into something beneficial. This simple determination has been one of the most powerful mindsets I've acquired, and over time it becomes second nature.

- A quote to live by: "No man ever sank under the burden of the day. It is when tomorrow's weight is added that the weight is more than a man can bear." —George McDonald

- Almost every survivor I've interviewed—and I've talked with over a hundred—mentioned how they celebrated the little steps they made, giving themselves a pat on the back. We would be fools not to follow their example when our situation looks dark or our mountain too high.

- Successful people ease stressful situations simply by telling themselves *I have done my best.* If you've done your best, you will never have regrets; you will never feel a sense of failure.

- If I find myself feeling like a victim, I say to myself, *I'm partly responsible for the situation in some small way, and I have the means to improve it—it is just going to take time.*

- To combat a helpless feeling, force yourself to take an initiative, no matter how seemingly insignificant. This transforms you from victim to survivor, fueling the tiny flame of confidence that will grow in time. Initiative, even that which doesn't yield the hoped-for results, reaffirms a sense of control. It's the simple *act of doing* that leads to a brighter outlook.

**CHAPTER 4**

# INTUITION

---

**"A list of pros and cons is not always as important as whether it feels right."**

—Deb Kiley

---

Deb Kiley had a vague sense of unease before her voyage on the *Trashman* with fellow crewmembers Brad Cavanaugh, Mark Adams, Meg Mooney, and Captain John Lippoth. She didn't get along with Mark, but there was something more, a pervasive gloomy feeling about sailing the *Trashman* from Maryland to Florida. Getting to Florida, however, was part of her plan, and she didn't give other methods of travel serious consideration. Deb figured the sail to Florida would be relatively brief, and then she'd leave the boat and be done with it.

Just one day before departure, however, Deb's gut feeling became more pronounced, telling her something wasn't quite right, and she decided against making the voyage. She called the boat's owner and told him she was backing out and resigning as one of the crew. He in turn reminded Deb of her commitment, and her resolve weakened. "Before the lecture [from the owner] was over, I knew I was not going to get out of this trip. I walked back to the boat feeling like a fool—for making the call and for being such a pushover."

She should have listened to her instincts and never made the trip. Prior to the voyage to Florida, she had spent several days on the boat with Captain John, and there had been a couple of warning signs she chose to ignore. Perhaps the biggest red flag occurred on the very first day she stepped foot on the vessel, when she followed John down into the galley. "Empty Heineken bottles covered nearly every flat surface and an open bag of potato chips was lying on the floor," she wrote in her book *Albatross*. There were other signals that neither the boat nor the captain were shipshape, but she let those slide, instead thinking ahead to the warm sunshine awaiting her in Florida, where she planned to spend the winter or sign on with another sailboat cruising the Caribbean.

As discussed earlier in this book, only Deb and Brad survived the sinking of the *Trashman* and the horrors that followed. Deb later said, "A list of pros and cons is not always as important as whether it feels right." We should all sear this one sentence into our heads, and heed its message, especially with big decisions or risky ventures.

One of the more heartbreaking instances of suppressing a gut feeling happened to Claudene Christian during Hurricane Sandy. Claudene was a crewmember on the tall ship *Bounty*, a replica of the original HMS *Bounty* made famous by the mutiny. The entire crew, including Claudene, agreed with the captain's decision to try to sail around the approaching hurricane. [We will examine the reasons *why* the crew agreed in a later chapter.] Claudene was a relatively new crewmember, and perhaps she followed the lead of the more seasoned sailors who believed they could safely get past the storm, which they all knew was incredibly powerful and coming their way.

The *Bounty* started its ill-fated voyage from New London, Connecticut with a destination of Florida. When the ship left port, Hurricane Sandy was in the Caribbean and its projected path was north, along the east coast of the US. This would put it on a collision course with the *Bounty*. But Robin Walbridge, captain of the *Bounty*, had maneuvered around hurricanes successfully in the past, and told the crew he could do so again.

Claudene's parents, who had been listening to weather reports about the burgeoning hurricane in the Atlantic, became quite concerned, and her mother, Dina, texted her daughter, asking her not to make the voyage. Claudene responded, "*Bounty* loves hurricanes, haven't you heard? The captain has thirty years' experience. All will be ok..."

Claudene might have been reassuring herself as much as her mother about her decision to sail.

*Bounty* left New London on Thursday evening, October 25, 2012, and on the ship's Facebook page the entry at 6:00 p.m. read, "*Bounty* will be sailing due East out to sea before heading South to avoid the brunt of Hurricane Sandy."

Shortly after the ship was underway, Claudene's concern, combined with an intuition that things would not go as planned, became clear. Her gut feeling of true danger surfaced far ahead of any problems that would later emerge on the ship. While most of the rest of the crew was looking forward to a bracing sail in strong winds, and relished the challenge to show their teamwork, Claudene confided her apprehension to a fellow crewmember: "The storm looks like it's going to be so enormous we are going to have to go halfway to Europe."

The uneasy feeling Claudene had only grew in strength—just like the hurricane steadily moving toward her. She decided to call her mother before cell phone reception was lost. "We are out on the ocean and I'm afraid I'm going to lose reception. I gotta tell you how much I love you, I really do." Moments later, she followed up the brief phone call with a haunting text. "If I go down with the ship and the worst happens, just know I am truly, genuinely happy."

Two days later, on Saturday October 27, Captain Walbridge, after digesting marine weather forecasts warning the hurricane was growing in size, decided to change course and head west, hopping to slip between Sandy and the US coast. This tactic made sense, as it would put the *Bounty* on the side of the hurricane where the winds have a bit less power. The move, however, would only work *if* they could cross in front of the hurricane without slowing down, similar to traversing railroad tracks with an oncoming train heading your way. You can get across safely if you don't stall. Unfortunately, on Sunday, October 28, *Bounty* was taking on more water than the pumps could handle, and soon she lost engine power altogether. Claudene's earlier feeling that something terrible would happen was now becoming a reality, and even the most optimistic crewmember knew they were in trouble.

Sandy grew to be the largest hurricane ever recorded, with storm force winds spanning an incredible 900 miles. And *Bounty*, wallowing in thirty-foot seas, was a sitting duck. In the dark early morning of Monday, October 29, with the crew in their survival suits and ready to abandon ship at first light, *Bounty* was suddenly knocked on her side by a huge wave. A near-miraculous Coast Guard rescue ensued, but tragically both Captain Robin Walbridge and Claudene Christian drowned.

Kathy Gilchrist, like Claudene Christian and Deb Kiley, felt a bit hesitant before the start of her voyage on the *Almeisan* with Loch Reidy, Tom Tighe, Chris Ferrer, and Ron Burd. She knew part of her sense of unease was due to the timing of the trip in early May, which she thought might be a bit early for a Connecticut-to-Bermuda sailing voyage. Where the rest of her sense of foreboding was coming from, she really didn't know. She had complete respect for the captain, because she had taken a sailing course that he taught, and she herself had been sailing countless times. And so she brushed aside her sense of misgiving.

That uneasy feeling, however, returned the day she arrived at the boat to begin the voyage, but she couldn't put her finger on the reason. Still, her anxiousness was strong enough that she considered telling the captain she'd decided not to go. Then she thought of how she'd committed to this trip, how the captain was counting on her, and she decided to keep her thoughts to herself. That turned out to be a mistake that almost cost Kathy her life. As chronicled earlier, the *Almeisan* and its crew of five were hammered by a storm so powerful that one wave capsized the boat, sweeping Kathy out of the cockpit. If not for the safety harness that tethered her to the boat, she surely would have died.

The same storm that Kathy was in also capsized the *At Ease*, with Bob Cummings and Jerry McCarthy onboard. When I interviewed Jerry, he told me a curious story regarding his mother. He explained how he'd logged over 250,000 sailing miles, and that his mother never feared for her son. But the night that Jerry and Bob's vessel capsized off North Carolina, his mother, living in Ireland, had a nightmare about Jerry being tossed about by huge seas. Even when she woke up, she could not shake her strong sense of concern for her son. Later that morning, she was watching television and a report mentioned that a powerful storm off the eastern seaboard of the United States had put several boats in jeopardy, one of which was called the *At Ease*. "Oh my God," shouted Mrs. McCarthy, "that's the boat Jerry is on!"

Deb, Claudene, Kathy, and Mrs. McCarthy all had an intuitive feeling that something was wrong. [The fact that all three are women may not be a coincidence—my researching of survival stories seems to indicate women are more in tune with this phenomenon. Dr. Helene Deutsch thinks the reason might be that, in adolescence, boys are fixating on asserting themselves through action, while girls' interests focus on their feelings and those of others.] In hindsight, the four women's senses of oncoming disaster were quite different. For Deb Kiley, it was the captain's lackadaisical manner. Claudene Christian had a powerful sense of doom, even though the rest of the crew did not. Kathy Gilchrist may not have been able to fully articulate her sense of hesitation, but whatever the reason, it was real. And for Mrs. McCarthy, it was a mother's intuition, which no one has ever clearly explained. Her premonition was more in the category of ESP and clairvoyance, which have been debated by scientists for years. Although I've never experienced such a sensation, I'm a firm believer that it happens. My primary interest, however, is in intuitive feelings—similar to Deb Kiley's—arising from meaningful observations that have been swept aside or overridden by the "rational" mind.

There are numerous cases of survivors who later reported they had a nagging feeling of trepidation before they embarked on a journey or an outing that they had done many times before without incident. So what is the basis for their gut feelings? I'm convinced that it is *the subconscious mind picking up clues that have not yet fully formed in our consciousness.* This is why it's so difficult for an individual experiencing the intuition to articulate why they feel the way they do. If the clue or clues have not yet percolated from the subconscious to the conscious mind, who could blame a person for dismissing an unspecific apprehension?

Premonitions, hunches, intuitions, a sixth sense—call it what you will, but realize that you ignore it at your peril. These feelings don't have to make perfect sense, because your subconscious mind is still working on the situation and has yet to connect the dots. Another way to look at your intuition is to view it as an early warning system. Logic and rationality certainly have their place, but the subconscious mind is vast, and it can assert itself in a very subtle way. It's up to us to be receptive to that mysterious sixth sense or presentiment.

The initial intuitive warning may be as simple as one factor in a familiar pattern being out of place or unusual, and your subconscious mind detecting a fleeting portent of a threat. But because we do not deliberately seek to recognize or acknowledge the aberration, it is dismissed. The vague, uneasy feeling is not clear-cut logic, and so is not taken seriously. Research psychologist Gary Klein explains that "Intuition has a strange reputation. Skilled decision makers know they can depend on their intuition, but at the same time they may feel uncomfortable trusting a source of power that seems so accidental."

To get beyond the trust issue, think of yourself as a detective. Some detectives excel at ferreting out clues that others have overlooked, just as some survivors are better than others noticing an uneasy feeling. And of course, intuition can also be a positive feeling, leading us to have that sense that *it just feels right*. Again, the clues are not fully formed, but there are enough positive ones burgeoning inside you that the resulting feeling is one of comfort and enthusiasm, even though you may not be able to articulate why. You will know the difference between intuition and fear because fear is emotionally charged, and it's a good bet it comes when you try something new or tackle something you have long been afraid of. Fear is often attached to past psychological wounds. Fear can lead to a jittery, nervous feeling, resulting in stress that is quite clear to you. Intuition, on the other hand, cannot be easily explained. It is focused on the present (rather than a longstanding fear) and is often directed at an activity you are normally comfortable with.

Intuition has been acknowledged by scientists, psychologists, and researchers throughout history. Albert Einstein said, "when you follow intuition, the solutions come to you and you don't know why." Author Gavin de Becker, in *The Gift of Fear*, writes that what people "dismiss as a gut feeling is in fact a cognitive process faster than we can recognize and far different than the familiar step by step thinking we rely on so willingly. We think conscious thought is somehow better when in fact intuition is soaring flight compared to prodding logic." Psychoanalyst Elizabeth Lloyd Mayer, in *Extraordinary Knowing*, suggests that we should be able to go back and forth between both rational and intuitive knowledge, and that someday we will train extrasensory perception to assist us in decision-making and knowing each other better.

Most people, however, are nowhere near the point of training their intuition, because they don't even acknowledge it. There is nothing concrete about it, no facts are apparent, and the voice of intuition is often a whisper. So the first step is to be receptive to that inner voice, no matter how quiet it is. With survivors, the voice they heard is a cautionary one, often nothing more than an uneasy sense. The key is that when we get that message, we need to stop and ask, "What could be making me feel uncomfortable?" We need to become focused on our surroundings, looking for signs that something is amiss, that something isn't quite right. This is the process of bringing those unconscious clues to the surface. It is not the same as acting on impulse. Rather, it is a gathering of all the information, looking at it from different angles, and then making a decision that feels right because it is in keeping with who you are. There is no procrastination, no drifting aimlessly, because not making a decision is *still making a decision*—it means you have decided on the status quo.

Consider a situation where you have a big decision to make, and you agonize over which way to go. You've gathered all the facts, tried your best to listen to your instinct (but felt nothing), and even discussed the issue with a trusted friend, yet still can't chose the best option. What do you do next? I have a friend who came up with her own little process to coax her gut feeling to the surface. When she truly could not decide on something important, she told herself she would abide by the outcome of a coin toss. The last time she did this, the issue was whether to take a new job that was offered to her. Heads meant she would take the job, and tails meant she would not. She flipped the coin and paid close attention to how she felt. "Heads came up," she said, "meaning take the new position. But now, for the first time, I felt my intuition. There was no feeling of relief or excitement about the decision to take the job. Finally, this was my intuition coming through, and I listened to it and did not take the job. I felt at peace with my decision."

By forcing the issue, my friend felt a strong and quick judgment, rather than the prior days of indecision. Like Deb Kiley, she could have made a list of pros and cons. It would not have been a wasted exercise, and it might have prompted more introspection about what appealed to her and what did not about the new job. However, she might have had ten "pros" and only two "cons," but those two cons might have carried much more weight in the category of whether they fit her core values, skill sets, and long-range goals. For example, is a job that pays her 20 percent more, has better benefits, and is a bit closer to home better than one offering more meaningful work? It's a difficult decision. Some people will go for the monetary benefits, but others will follow that intuitive feeling that the more consequential work will, at the end of the day, lead to long-term happiness.

Author Gerd Gigerenzer, in *Gut Feelings*, believes that gut feelings are rules of thumb which take advantage of evolved capacities of the brain and are superior to a complex weighing of pros and cons. "A rule of thumb is quite different from a balance sheet with pros and cons: it tries to hit at the most important information and ignores the rest."

Another technique, a bit different than my friend's coin toss, is to sit quietly and imagine you have made a decision you have agonized over. Do you feel peaceful? Is there a calm feeling welling up? Then imagine you have made the opposite decision, and compare those sensations. Are your shoulders tensing up? Is your throat tightening? If these feelings are generally negative, you probably are not comfortable with the decision, but you still have work to do. Could your negative feelings be coming from a similar situation that did not work out in the past? Stop and think how this new situation differs, and if it has entirely unique variables, maybe you need to consider that the unpleasant feeling you are getting is because of a past trauma, which has little connection to the new situation.

Finally, if none of these techniques help you make a crucial judgment, there is one last step to take. This may not work in every situation, but given the option, *choose the decision that is reversible.* That way, if the feeling of dread exerts itself when you are moving down the path you chose, you can turn back. There is no permanent damage or "Well, I can't turn back now."

My friend Hugh Bishop, one of the pioneers of far-offshore lobster fishing, related a story where an intuitive feeling caused him to do something that overrode what his "brain" was instructing him to do. He and his crew were over a hundred miles out to sea, hauling traps, when a thick fog moved in. As always, he had his boat's radar on, which could extend to a range of twenty-four miles. Hugh checked it often on this day because of the fog.

It was a productive trip, and after lunch the men took a short break before hauling again. Hugh took an eight-minute nap, and when he awoke, his first thought was, *I better check the radar again.* But instead of going to the pilothouse, he stayed below and moved toward the head, where there was a little escape hatch to the outer deck. In his book *Marblehead's First Harbor* he wrote, "For some unknown reason, I started walking forward, away from the pilothouse and the radar." Hugh asked himself, *Why are you walking forward? You won't see anything up there today.* The naked eye could not see more than twenty-five yards in the fog, while the radar covered miles in all directions. But Hugh's feet, as if they had a mind of their own, were taking him in the direction of the little hatch, and he let them lead the way.

Once at the hatch, Hugh stuck his head out. "I heard something I'll never forget. It was the distinct sound water makes in the form of breaking waves. At that instant, looking toward the sound, I saw the bow of a very large vessel. Near the waterline I saw rust, but a few feet higher the bow, all black, disappeared up into the fog."

The enormous vessel was bearing down on Hugh's lobster boat and would run them down within seconds. Hugh ran to the pilothouse and threw the gear shift lever into reverse and gave the engine full throttle. He looked out the window and saw nothing but the oncoming enormous black hull of the ship, and waited for the impact.

The vessel, Hugh recalled, passed within inches. It was a 900-foot container ship that would have obliterated the lobster boat. Hugh said it took many years to even talk about this incident. "What made me walk forward? If I had I gone up to look at the radar, by the time my eyes had adjusted, we would have been run through. Call it whatever you want, but something was with me that day that was awfully powerful."

Can we always count on getting a gut feeling? No. One of the more well-known examples is fisherman Adam Randall, whose intuition kept him off the *Andrea Gail* fishing boat that was chronicled in *The Perfect Storm*. Randall had driven a couple hours from his home in East Bridgewater, Massachusetts, to Gloucester with his father-in-law, to leave on the fishing trip that very day. When he got out of the car, some strong feeling came over him. We know it wasn't the vessel because Randall knew boats, was familiar with the *Andrea Gail*, and he felt it was well-built. Nor were there misgivings about his crewmates, because he knew most of them. But Randall had a funny feeling, a bad vibe, and he acted on it. He got back in his father-in-law's car and told him he was not going to go on the trip. Whatever premonition he had was accurate, because the *Andrea Gail* disappeared without a trace in a monster storm several days later.

Premonitions, or whatever you want to call such feelings, don't always come knocking when they should. Just a few months after Randall aborted his trip on the *Andrea Gail*, he signed up to crew on the *Terri Lei*, out of South Carolina. No one knows exactly what happened, but an EPIRB was activated on the *Terri Lei*, after just a couple days out at sea. When rescuers arrived, they found debris and an empty life raft, but the vessel and the entire crew were gone.

Ironically, listening to our intuition can feel counterintuitive! All our lives, we have been trained to gather facts to support a decision, yet with intuition we have no hard facts, and we either discount our hunch or suppress it. We also have been trained, going back to elementary school, to listen to the teacher and learn by memorizing. We are seldom encouraged to ask questions and poke holes in the prevailing wisdom. Yet, when it comes to intuition, asking questions is essential to get at the source of our feelings. Remember, if we believe that most intuition is caused by clues in the subconscious mind, it's our job to try to bring those clues to the surface by probing and asking questions such as, *Why do I feel uneasy? Is there something here I'm missing? Do I really trust this person? Is this situation one in which I could be trapped? Did that person say something a while back that caused me to question their judgment? Have I read something about this scenario a long time ago that is making me uncomfortable?* These are the types of questions that can bring the feeling from the gut to the brain. But first, we must be receptive to receiving subliminal messages and not dismiss them out of hand.

We place an inordinate reliance on our vision, focusing on what we see rather than what our subconscious mind or instinct is telling us. But an animal never discounts a sense of fear. Most animals, even when they cannot see, hear, or smell danger, seem to sense it first. And they freeze, waiting to confirm the source of their fear. Then they decide if the threat is serious, and they flee, or, if the threat never materializes, they move on. We should learn to do the same. Intuition is nature's way of protecting us when we might be at risk.

Learning to connect to our intuition and process clues, emotions, and subliminal messages isn't easy, and it takes some work and time. Yet the payoff can save you from putting yourself in situations you later regret. Too many of us suppress feelings that cannot be articulated and readily supported by facts, only to later learn our gut feeling was more accurate than our rational brain or our list of pros and cons.

# SURVIVOR LESSONS FOR YOUR LIFE:

- Intuition, I believe, is not some mysterious or mystic phenomenon. It is subconscious clues that you can't yet articulate, but that can help guide you. Oftentimes, after the event occurs, you realize exactly what those clues were all about.

- Deb Kiley's observation is succinct and on target: "A list of pros and cons is not always as important as whether it feels right."

- View your intuition as an early warning system. Logic and rationality certainly have their place, but the subconscious mind is vast, and it can assert itself in a very subtle way. It's up to us to be receptive to that mysterious sixth sense or presentiment.

- You will know the difference between intuition and fear because fear is emotionally charged, and it's a good bet it comes when you try something new or tackle something you have long been afraid of. The stress from fear is quite clear to you. Intuition, on the other hand, cannot be easily explained. It is focused on the present (rather than a longstanding fear), and is often directed at an activity you are normally comfortable with.

- "When you follow intuition, the *solutions* come to you and you don't know why." —Albert Einstein

- When you have a vague sense of unease, ask yourself, "What could be making me feel uncomfortable?" We need to become focused on our surroundings, looking for signs that something is amiss, that something isn't quite right.

- Given the option, chose the decision that is reversible.

- If you have a decision you're agonizing over, sit quietly and imagine you have made a decision: X. Do you feel peaceful? Is there a calm feeling welling up? Then imagine you have made the opposite decision, and compare those sensations. You now have the first indication about which way to go, but don't shy away from something strictly because of fear, and instead, take time to examine why you feel a certain way. The old saying "sleep on it" makes sense. Delay making the decision for a day or two, and new clues may percolate to the surface.

- In summary, be receptive to receiving subliminal messages and don't dismiss them out of hand. Then stop and try to ascertain why you feel a certain way. This two-step process is not always easy, but once you get in the habit of implementing it, decisions become easier.

## CHAPTER 5

# HELP FROM WITHIN & BEYOND

"There are energies larger than we are that surround us everywhere, and when the times are right, we can connect with those energies."

—Aron Ralston

"The voice was clean and sharp and commanding. It was always right…"

—Joe Simpson

"We were not alone out there."

—Bernie Webber

Many people in dire circumstances report that they were helped by an outside force or higher power. Some called the entity God, some said it was a universal spirit or guardian angel, and others were certain it was a deceased friend or loved one. All reported that they felt an external presence at their most vulnerable moment, and that this mysterious force was helping, encouraging, and guiding them to safety. There is even a term for this phenomenon, "The Third Man." Originating in T. S. Eliot's poem *The Waste Land*, it was inspired by an unusual event during the epic survival ordeal of Ernest Shackleton and crew.

Near the end of Shackleton's sixteen-month tribulation in the Antarctic, he and two of his companions were making one last desperate push to scale frozen mountains toward safety and return with help for the rest of his crew. Shackleton and his men had already traveled hundreds of miles by foot and small boat, and were near the very end of their endurance after going for months with insufficient food and shelter.

Shackleton later explained that, at his lowest moment, it seemed that there was one additional man trudging alongside him, encouraging him to push onward. The mysterious presence could not be explained by the explorer, but whatever it was, Shackleton was grateful that it was there. His two companions, Frank Worsley and Tom Crean, also felt this guiding presence of another being. This extra person would have been the fourth man, but T. S. Eliot used poetic license and referred to this unseen being as the "third" one of the group (rather than the fourth), and that term stuck.

Shackleton was reluctant to talk about this, but when he did, he said, "I have no doubt that Providence guided us."

Author John Geiger, in his book *The Third Man Factor*, delves into this phenomenon, citing dozens of examples where a seen or unseen presence helped an individual who was close to death conquer that final barrier in their path to safety. Many of the survivors who experienced this "Third Man" are quite well known:

- Charles Lindbergh, during his trans-Atlantic flight: "vaguely outlined forms...reassuring me...At times, voices come out of the air itself...giving me messages of importance unattainable in ordinary life."

- Joshua Slocum, in his around-the-world solo voyage: "I saw a tall man at the helm (who said) 'I have come to help you.'"

- Frank Smythe, on his climb near the top of Mount Everest: "All the time I was climbing alone, I had a strong feeling that I was accompanied by another."

Even my personal hero John Muir, when trapped on a sheer rock wall on Mount Ritter, felt a "presence" that "came forward and assumed control."

When I interviewed Black Hawk helicopter pilot Bob Cummings about a capsizing on his sailboat while he was on leave from the US Army, I was surprised when he matter-of-factly mentioned that a "voice" had saved his life. Cummings had seen combat in Operation Desert Storm in Iraq, and his twenty-year career as a military pilot made him uniquely qualified to assess risk. He recalled the storm he was in on his sailboat was one of the most dangerous situations he'd ever been in, and that the voice was as clear as day. Cummings was trapped underwater when a giant wave overturned his sailboat, and he was about to unclip his safety harness when the "Third Man" said in a firm voice, "If you release, you will die."

Both Cummings and Muir attributed their survival to that key moment when something beyond themselves either took control or pointed out the correct course of action.

Cummings's experience with a "voice" might sound highly unusual, but I've come across it countless times, either interviewing survivors or during research. An example is from Ina Downs, who was on a ship that was torpedoed forty miles off New Orleans by a German U-boat in 1942. Ina later recorded an audio tape about her survival experience, and said that when the ship was torpedoed, she clung to a perch, afraid of entering the dark ocean alone at 2:00 a.m. Then, out of the blue, a calm but stern voice simply said, "Jump or you'll go down with the ship." She pushed away from the ship, despite her fears, and dropped through the blackness of night into the void of the ocean below.

The ship Ina was on, the *Heredia*, sank and would have sucked Ina into the depths. Her ordeal was far from over, but by listening to the voice, she escaped the torpedoed ship and spent the night floating in the ocean. The lowest point in her eighteen hours of bobbing alone in the ocean occurred when she felt a bump against her leg. She peered down into the water and saw several small pilot fish. But then she spotted something much larger that made her gasp. A shark! She glanced around her and now saw the fins of other sharks lazily cutting through the ocean's surface, circling her.

She prayed to God to either save her or make her death a speedy one. Within minutes, the sharks moved off, apparently losing interest in Ina. Night fell, and she was terrified the sharks would return. An hour later, the voice that had told her to jump from the ship gave her another instruction: "Look up in front of you."

She saw a light not far away, and she began shouting for help. The light came toward her, and now Ina could see another light, a searchlight sweeping the ocean. A shrimp trawler slowly motored her way, and soon she was hauled on board.

Maybe the sensation of the presence of another being during a harrowing ordeal is a part of our brain we have never tapped before, and only asserts itself in the most desperate of times. Mountaineer Joe Simpson discussed a "voice" telling him what to do after he fell into a deep crevasse and was left for dead. Simpson severely injured his lower leg when the impact from the fall drove the bones of his leg through his knee joint. His only hope of survival was to crawl backward for several agonizing miles of a crevasse-filled glacier through a killing zone at high altitude.

With no food or water, his chances of living were remote indeed, which he later acknowledged: "My abiding memory is of an appalling sense of loneliness.... I wanted to be with somebody when I died." Incredibly, after three days of crawling, he made it to base camp. He credits his feat to an insistent voice that prodded him. "The voice," said Simpson, "was clean and sharp and commanding. It was always right...Reaching the glacier was my aim, the voice told me exactly how to go about it, and I obeyed while my other mind jumped abstractedly from one idea to another."

Simpson's "voice" could have been a higher power, something outside of himself, or it could have been the wise man within. We will never know, but it saved the mountaineer's life. At one point in his crawl to safety, he was desperate for sleep. "Don't sleep, don't sleep, not here," said the voice. "Keep going, find a slope and dig a snow hole." Simpson did just that, but the voice soon woke him: "Get moving...don't lie there...stop dozing...move!"

It was as if Simpson had sprouted a second brain, and this one knew what must be done for ultimate survival. Whatever the voice was, it worked. When Simpson crawled into base camp, he had lost one third of his body weight, but he was alive.

In his book *Alone*, R. Logan delves into dozens of cases of survivors being instructed by a commanding voice or presence that helps them make the right decisions during their ordeals. These people swore the voices were not from within, nor were they hallucinating. Logan's study focused on survivors who faced prolonged solitary ordeals, and one wonders if the mind conjures up these "Third Man" scenarios to help offset the isolation during lengthy periods of extreme duress.

I've also interviewed survivors who have heard a commanding voice or felt the presence of the third man in short periods of survival. One of those was Josh Scornavacchi, who slid off the *Bounty* when it capsized and found himself trapped underwater, tangled in lines from the ship.

Josh could feel his life force leaving him as his lungs screamed for air. Then a clear voice said, "It's not your time yet." A second later, he was free from the tangle of lines and swam to the surface. His ordeal was far from over, but the voice did not leave him. To get away from the suction of the sinking ship, which lay on its side, he grabbed hold of the mizzenmast and tried to pull himself up from the debris in the water. As waves pounded *Bounty*, the mast started rising from the water, taking Josh up with it. He clung to the mast as it rose, but the voice shouted at him to do the opposite. "Jump!" commanded the voice. Josh didn't want to jump, but he did as instructed, and landed in a clear patch of water not far from a life raft canister.

Could the voice have been another crew member? Josh said no: the shrieking wind made it impossible to be heard unless you were speaking right in the face of another person. Certainly the first voice telling him "It's not your time" could not have been from a crewmember because Josh was underwater.

Maybe the voice that commanded Josh to jump was from the deepest recesses of his rational brain, overruling the mind-body connection that wanted him to hold onto the mast that took him out of the water? We will never know, but it seems that in all the examples of a voice coming from somewhere outside oneself, the voice is looking at long-term survival, overruling the immediate needs of the body. That was clearly the case with Josh and with Joe Simpson, when he so desperately wanted to sleep.

Aron Ralston, who cut his arm off when pinned by a boulder, went out of his way in the acknowledgement section of his book to never forget "the awe-inspiring power of the greater spirit." His view is that "there are energies larger than we are that surround us everywhere, and when the times are right, we can connect with those energies." Most survivors would concur.

To my way of thinking, it really doesn't matter whether these encounters were real or whether they were brought on by imagination, sleep deprivation, isolation, dehydration, or trauma. What is important is to know is that during times of extreme duress, we may very well get help from an unlikely source, and we should keep an open mind to allow this comfort to come our way. And if during a time of survival you hear a voice, don't dismiss it out of hand. There are simply too many survivors who credit the voice with saving their lives.

Bernie Webber, perhaps the Coast Guard's most famous hero, described to me how he felt a divine presence during his mission that was so audacious it later became a Disney movie. Although there was no "voice," he explained that the presence was just as real, and it guided him in his decision-making. His daring feat occurred on February 18, 1952, when he and three crewmembers were sent on what Bernie thought was a suicide rescue attempt. The assignment was so dangerous that his every move could have a life-or-death consequence, no different than the extreme survivors we've profiled. A powerful Nor'easter had whipped the ocean off Cape Cod into mountainous sixty-foot seas. Webber was ordered to take out the thirty-six-foot wooden lifeboat and search for the stern section of a 500-foot oil tanker that the seas had split in half. To make matters worse, this order came at dusk, and to reach the open ocean, Webber would have to pilot the boat over the dreaded Chatham Bar, where incoming rollers are forced upward by the shallow waters of the bar.

Webber knew that the waves at the bar become so steep they collapse upon themselves, and would avalanche down on his little wooden boat, potentially causing it to capsize. And should that happen, Webber and crew would either be dead from either immediate drowning, or possibly last another five minutes before they succumbed to hypothermia.

As the thirty-six-foot boat approached the foaming seas of the Chatham Bar, Webber used his radio to contact Chatham Coast Guard Station, hoping his commander might change his mind and tell him to return to port. Instead, his commander said, "Proceed as directed."

The four Coast Guardsmen could clearly hear the thundering of the waves at the bar over the shrieking wind. By now, night had cloaked the ocean in darkness, and the crew could only see a few feet in front of them with the aid of a tiny searchlight. They knew this might be their last couple of minutes alive. And then they did something odd. As if on cue, they started to sing "Rock of Ages," perhaps to steady their nerves, or perhaps in defiance of the sea. Each man had a different feeling, but all four sang along.

The first breaking wave to hit the boat blew out the windshield directly in front of Webber, and the torrents of water poured into the cockpit, tearing the compass off its mount. They had lost their sole means of navigation. Even worse, they had lost engine power.

Engineer Andy Fitzgerald slid down into the engine room, re-primed the motor, hit the electric start, and the engine coughed back to life. That would have been my cue to turn back to safety. Webber, however, turned the vessel back into the oncoming seas and, giving the boat full throttle, punched his way through the next giant wave. Those four young Coasties then made the stuff of maritime legend, by rescuing thirty-two out of thirty-three men on the sinking half-tanker.

I interviewed Bernie many years later, and during our first conversation he said, "If you write about this rescue, you have to make it clear that it wasn't just me and the crew that got us through that night. We were divinely guided, and of that I'm sure. I felt it. There is no other explanation of how we got over the Chatham Bar, found the section of tanker in the dark, crammed our tiny lifeboat with an additional thirty-two men, and made it back to port in such chaotic seas. There were also several events prior to this rescue that I think specifically happened to help me that night. We were not alone out there."

While some survivors feel a connection to a higher power, God, or a third man, almost all survivors I've met and researched knew that they had to do their part and not just pray and hope. Robert Byrd in

*Alone* said it best: "And yet, being a practical man, I recognized a big difference between the mere affirmation of faith and its effective implementation." He knew he needed to combine his desire to be in God's grace with his own actions to stay alive.

By no means is it necessary to be part of any religion to get through an ordeal. Maurice and Maralyn Bailey survived 117 days adrift at sea. Maralyn later wrote, "I have never followed any religion and the isolation and insecurity did not bring any form of conversion." Maralyn simply did not want to die, and was going to do everything in her power to keep living because there was so much she still wanted to do and see. She had her own belief system: "Each happening in our lives prepares us for some eventual test." Maralyn believed in both fate and our ability to "write our own future." By applying unwavering determination, Maralyn felt each of us can help shape outcomes to reach our full destiny.

Ernie Hazard had a similar view, knowing he played the pivotal role in determining his fate. He thought the time for thinking and thanking God, or whatever higher power is out there, should come *after* his rescue. Ernie felt very strongly that he had to be 100 percent focused on how to help himself. While the Baileys were adrift for many days and used the solitude for introspection, most of Ernie's fifty hours in the life raft were focused on just surviving the next fifteen minutes, as he was in seas of sixty feet and frigid temperatures. Ernie later joked to me that God had more serious problems to focus on than his. But Ernie also didn't want to let his guard down for a single minute, or weaken his resolve by hoping for a miracle. He knew that, prior to his boat capsizing, there had been no time for a Mayday, and consequently it would be many hours before the Coast Guard was alerted that a boat was missing. Rescue was a long shot, but his approach was to still be alive when and if the Coast Guard came. In other words, "be ready."

Lochlin Reidy, like Ernie, did not spend time praying, because he too was thinking *be ready*. In fact, those two words became his mantra during his time in the ocean. Loch's spiritual beliefs don't fall neatly into one religion. He thinks there is something in the universe more complex and powerful than any of us can imagine, but whatever that energy is, it was not necessarily aware or concerned about his predicament. *You've got to do your part,* Loch would tell himself, *and the Coast Guard will do theirs.*

Loch's situation was different from Ernie's because his boat's EPIRB had been activated and his captain had issued a Mayday. However, rescue would be difficult because he was more than 300 nautical miles from land. But he never doubted that the Coast Guard would be searching, and he had faith that their search plan would be thorough and complete. He simply had to stay alive until either a ship, plane, or helicopter was in the area, and then he had to be ready to signal it with his two-inch strobe light.

For people like Loch, Ernie, and Maralyn Bailey, relying on something beyond themselves was not as important as making the most of their own resourcefulness. For them, it was essential to feel they were devoting every thought and every ounce of energy to their survival. This gave them a small measure of control in a chaotic circumstance where so much was out of their hands.

Other survivors hold a strong belief that God will help them, but only if the survivor does his part. In other words, they were not going to passively wait for a miracle. Captain Eddie Rickenbacker, a Medal of Honor recipient and fighter pilot ace, used this combination of help from beyond and within when the bomber he was on with eight crewmen crash-landed in the Pacific. The men were able to exit the plane and board two tiny life rafts that only had enough food and water for three days. But under Rickenbacker's leadership, all but one of the castaways managed to stay alive for twenty-four days before rescue. The captain led his men in prayer: "You, our father, know we are not asking you to do it all. We will help ourselves if you give us a chance." Rickenbacker later explained he was not a religious man, but had enough faith in himself and God to be certain they would make it. When asked if he was a member of any religion, he said, "I do sort of have a religion of my own: I hold to the Golden Rule.... If a man just follows what he knows and feels is in his heart, then he can't go far wrong and is possessed of religion enough..."

Nando Parrado, who survived a horrific airplane crash in the Andes Mountains, pointed out the problem of putting too much faith in a higher power. Trapped on the glacier with the wrecked plane for over two months, Parrado watched others in the group slowly give up while praying for miracles. "They languished in the shadows of the fuselage, tortured by fears of dying, with their eyes dull and hollow, they were becoming ghosts already." Parrado tried shouting at them, summoning them to join in the common fight to survive, but to no effect. He decided that survivors were breaking because they were used to certainty, and now there was none.

This point was driven home to Parrado when he observed his friend Marcelo sinking into total despair. In his book *Miracle in the Andes*, Parrado described how, for Marcelo, "the world was an orderly place watched over by a wise and loving God." Parrado explained how his friend's faith was now working against him. "Marcelo had been broken not because his mind was weak, but because it was too strong. His faith in the rescue was absolute and unyielding: *God would not abandon us. The authorities would never leave us here to die.*" But when it was clear there would be no rescue, Marcelo's unshakable faith "now prevented him from adjusting to the blow and finding a new balance. His certainty, which had served him so well in the ordinary world, now robbed him of the balance and flexibility he needed to adjust to the strange new rules by which we were battling for our lives."

Observing Marcelo's willpower crumbling forced Parrado to change his normal way of thinking in the civilized world, and replace that with acceptance of total uncertainty. He taught himself to live moment to moment, so that nothing would surprise him, and so that his fears would not block his instinct to take action and risks.

If he stayed with the others who huddled in parts of the wrecked plane for shelter, they would all eventually be dead. Parrado decided he had nothing to lose by attempting what seemed near impossible: climb out of the Andes. He and another friend did just that on a grueling ten-day struggle that ultimately led to their salvation.

Perhaps the best way to fight through an overwhelming challenge is to use a combination of resources according to your own beliefs. Instead of asking God to change the situation or perform a miracle, ask him to give you the strength and wisdom to work through the problem. That way you acknowledge responsibility for finding the solutions, but know that you are not alone.

## SURVIVOR LESSONS FOR YOUR LIFE:

- Maralyn Bailey had her own simple belief: that through sheer determination, each of us can help shape our future. Turn off the part of your brain that tells you you're a victim, and activate the part that says you can influence whatever situation you find yourself in.

- Draw upon your individual faith to know that, in some mysterious way, your burden can be shared.

- Be open-minded about receiving reassurance and guidance from a higher power when you feel overwhelmed.

- Remember Rickenbacker's and Nando Parrado's maxim that you have to do your part and not rely solely on a higher power.

- Maybe the sensation of the presence of another being—the third man—during a harrowing ordeal is a part of our brain we have never tapped before, and only asserts itself in the most desperate of times. It really doesn't matter whether the examples of a "voice" were real or imagined. The voice may be the wise man buried deep in all of us that never panics. The important thing is to know that during times of extreme duress, we may very well get help from an unlikely source, and we should be receptive to allowing this comfort to come our way.

- The concept that extreme survivors have of "writing their own future" and "being ready" for help can be used by all of us on difficult journeys. We have to always be on the lookout for the little opportunities, otherwise we might miss the one that puts us over the finish line.

- Nando Parrado's acceptance of uncertainty helped save his life. We can improve our lives by acknowledging that life is full of uncertainty, and even embracing this uncertainty with the conviction that we will solve each problem as it happens. This mindset helps shield us from crumbling when the unforeseen happens.

## CHAPTER 6

# ENDURING: PEP TALKS, PATS ON THE BACK, & THE POSSIBILITY OF LUCK

"Having made up my mind that my time was not up, though needing to reassure myself on this point on several occasions, I proceeded to let my mind wander at will…"

—Douglas Wardrop

Falling off a ship in the middle of the Pacific Ocean at night—and having none of your shipmates hear your cries—is about as bad as it gets for survivability. Imagine watching the stern light on the ship slowly fade away over the wave tops as you tread water: no life raft, no life jacket, not even a flare.

That was the situation Douglas Wardrop found himself in on June 9, 1957, long before the advent of GPS, EPIRBs, and other modern devices that might have ultimately helped in his rescue. Wardrop was a twenty-three-year-old watch officer aboard the freighter *British Monarch*. The accident happened when he was checking the log clock that hung over the stern of the ship. Realizing an electrical component was malfunctioning he began to clean the connection. That's when an ocean swell caused Wardrop to lose his grip on a deck bracket and go tumbling overboard. His shouts for help were drowned out by the churning propeller, and he was left alone in the void.

Extreme survivors focus on what they can control, but Wardrop, dressed only in shirt, shorts, and shoes, had nothing to work with other than his thoughts. And now he was a thousand miles from land in an area of the Pacific where he hadn't seen another ship for many hours. He knew the odds of a rescue were the longest of long shots, but the sailor decided to push that thought aside and instead cling to the hope that eventually his crewmates would realize he was missing and the ship would return. But how to keep that thought paramount and not dwell on all the many reasons rescue was unlikely? Wardrop used what I call inner pep talks. He later described how he did it.

"Having made up my mind that my time was not up, though needing to reassure myself on this point on several occasions, I proceeded to let my mind wander at will, ignoring the body until the return of the ship."

Wardrop tried floating on his back, only to have swells wash over his face, so he fell into a rhythm of treading water with his feet and using his arms to slowly breaststroke. Then there was nothing to do but wait. He used that time to visualize the steps his shipmates would take to save him. First, they must realize he had disappeared. Waldrop calculated there was a chance he would be missed at breakfast or maybe when he failed to set the chronometer. He knew his fate was not just in the hands of his crewmates, but more importantly, the ship's captain, William Coutts.

Douglas Reeman, author of *Against the Sea*, described Wardrop's mindset: "Captain Coutts would turn back. Of course he would. Never for an instant could he [Wardrop] allow himself to doubt that. Coutts would do all he could to find him. All, that is, that was reasonable. Wardrop closed his mind to any deeper analysis."

Instead, the castaway pictured the scene on the ship once they learned of his disappearance. He considered the anxiety of the captain as he ordered the ship to turn around, along with the stress on the radio man. "I could visualize," wrote Wardrop, "the Radio

Officer sitting for hours in a small cabin surrounded by instruments, perspiration streaming off him, sending out frantic signals for all ships in the area to keep a sharp lookout..."

Treading water in the dark was accompanied by other discomforts, such as a stinging jellyfish, so Wardrop directed his thoughts to more comforting scenes. He recalled his days as a boy in school and that led him to conjure up his deceased father. Suddenly he heard his father's voice: "Come on, Doug, keep it up, you can do it."

Whether that was his father speaking to him or his own inner fortitude, the pep talk was just what Wardrop needed, and he even managed to enjoy the sunrise over the gray seas. The young sailor was doing his best to endure, clinging to the notion that, if he hung on long enough, his captain and crew would find him.

Think about it. If you are adrift in an endless ocean, why not fight on with the hope of rescue, and why not do it in the most positive way possible? Even if you are deluding yourself about the odds for rescue, that's okay—the goal is to go as long as you can and preserve your sanity in the process. Luck plays a role in so many rescues, why not help it along by being alive and ready when rescuers come searching?

While Wardrop did his part to let time pass and keep his spirits up, those on the ship were doing precisely what the sailor had imagined. After searching the ship, his crewmates and captain knew the awful truth that the young sailor had gone overboard in the middle of the night. Captain Coutts had no illusions that retracing their course and finding Wardrop would be anything less than a miracle, but he was a skilled navigator and he had to try, just as Wardrop knew he would.

As the hours went by and Wardrop expended precious energy treading water, he kept returning to positive reinforcements about rescue, continually imagining the ship returning and the crew on the lookout for him. He supplemented that with drawing strength from God and interpreting even the formation of clouds as having meaning. The sailor later described how one cloud looked like "a huge hand with index finger pointing in the general direction in which the ship will return. A coincidence? I hardly think so. Gazing at this cloud returns my thoughts to those on board. The members of the crew will now be posted at various vantage points throughout the ship, each watching and waiting with their own private thoughts..."

When a large sea turtle swam to his side, Waldrop rejoiced at the company. "My constant companion was a turtle of large dimensions, although unable to speak, he afforded me quite a few laughs at times. A very friendly chap he was..." The sailor spoke to the turtle as he would a dear friend and explained that he had fallen overboard, and that his mates would be searching, saying, "They won't be long now."

The turtle calmed Waldrop, and he soon fell asleep, dreaming that he was holding onto the rail of a hitching post. When he woke, he concluded he had actually been clutching the turtle's shell in his sleep and not a hitching post. He thanked the turtle for staying close.

Not long after he awoke, Wardrop saw his ship, the *British Monarch*. But would those onboard see him?

The castaway thought of the sailor on board with the sharpest eye, Mac Taylor, and he visualized Mac picking out his tiny bobbing head from the endless sea. Wardrop used his arms to splash water, so Mac would have a bigger target to locate.

Wardrop's pep talks and visualizations paid off. The ship came closer, lowered a launch, and his mates picked him up, explaining it was Mac Taylor who had spotted him. There was certainly good fortune involved: Captain Coutts later admitted it was at least 25 percent luck that they found the castaway. But Wardrop was the key. By not giving up, and instead bolstering his fighting spirit with inner conversations, searching for positive signs [the clouds], and even finding humor [his talk with the turtle], the young man did his part to stay optimistic and keep himself alive until salvation.

Almost every survivor I've interviewed or researched has said they encouraged themselves with positive reinforcement throughout their ordeal. They did so by either talking to themselves out loud, or having inner conversations where they gave themselves pats on the back, congratulations, or an inner dialogue of support.

Loch Reidy, whose ordeal at sea [keeping his captain's body with him] we examined earlier, constantly reminded himself while adrift to "be ready, the Coast Guard will come." He never thought "if" the Coast Guard arrived, but instead convinced himself throughout his suffering that the Coast Guard was first mobilizing resources and then actively searching. Over and over he kept repeating his mantra to not give up, but instead be as alert as possible to help in his own rescue. In his darkest hours, alone at night, Loch put a positive spin on the situation, thinking his strobe light would be more clearly seen in the dark, when [not if] help arrived.

Like Wardrop, Loch used cloud formations as positive reinforcement. Whether it was wishful thinking or a sign from the universe or higher power, it didn't really matter to Loch. What was important is that a particular cloud configuration gave him a boost to continue his struggle in chaotic seas of twenty to thirty feet. First the clouds seemed to form the "OK" sign a person makes with their thumb and forefinger, and then the clouds reshaped to look like a helicopter. Loch told himself to focus on the positive feeling the clouds briefly imparted. He instinctively knew that if he concentrated on encouraging and affirmative thoughts, they would assist him in keeping the negative ones at bay. Also similar to Wardrop's actions, Loch used beneficial visualizations, keeping the image of his rescue foremost in his mind. *A Coast Guard helicopter and airplane are already searching,* he told himself.

A few hours after Loch extracted comfort from the clouds, he saw a ship in the distance. As it steamed away, he realized he should have been swiveling his head at the tops of the bigger waves to try and spot ships early on. But rather than berate himself, Loch went into pep-talk mode. *You've got to always be ready. I'm going to make it. That ship was looking for me. Don't give up. Help could come at any moment.*

Loch didn't have a turtle to talk to as Wardrop did, but he did talk to a bird that hovered directly overhead, telling it to "go find help for us." And for humor, Loch used sarcasm when a wave hit him from an entirely new direction, slapping him directly in the face. "Oh nice," said Loch to the wave, "now you're coming at me from all sides!" He also used a mix of sarcasm and optimism when he started to worry about a shark arriving, telling himself, *No shark in its right mind would be swimming near the surface in these conditions.*

We hear "stay positive" all the time, but it's easier said than done when adversity is beating you down. Extreme survivors teach us that the way to maintain a positive outlook despite hardship is to first search for even the slightest glimmer of promise, and cling tightly to it. Wardrop and Loch found theirs in cloud formations and using their minds to visualize that their rescue was in progress. Equally important, they often verbalized their pep talks, and they did so at regular intervals. The process wasn't easy, and they had their setbacks, with Loch describing how his emotions would rise and fall just like the waves. He described pulling himself up from low points by reminding himself that it would be just a matter of time before he was located, and he needed to do his part to be ready.

Ernie Hazard, whose vessel was hit by the ninety-foot rogue wave, is the perfect case study for the power of pep talks and pats on the back. He described to me using certain phrases over and over, sometimes talking out loud and other times repeating the words in his mind. "Ride it out, just ride it out," was one of his mantras, while another was, "I can take this. Just hang on a little longer." The repetition of such statements helped intensify his determination.

These deliberate efforts at affirmation and encouragement are especially needed when a person is facing the ordeal alone, as Ernie, Loch, and Wardrop experienced. There is no shared suffering, no comradeship, and no spirit-boosting talk from others. The internal pep talk is crucial when fighting a battle all alone. Ernie, however, added another component: the all-important pat on the back, congratulating himself whenever he performed a task that helped his situation. "Good job, Ernie," he told himself more than once, "you're doing just fine."

There is an important distinction between accepting the situation and resigning yourself to its bleak, probable outcome. Ernie never denied his new reality, and he knew the odds were long to survive in the North Atlantic in late November in a leaky life raft. But he was determined to do little things to help his odds, and to do that he needed to tear himself from his occasional periods of despair through pep talks. At one point he prodded himself by saying, "Come on Hazard, keep it going. Don't go soft now. Roll with the punches, keep doing what you're doing." And those few words steeled him to endure another hour of his nightmare.

Ernie knew he had inner reserves of power that could be tapped, and he thought of himself as a fighter in a ring squaring off against the ocean that was pummeling him with breaking waves. When his frustration over his predicament boiled over, he even angrily shouted a challenge to the sea, "Is that the best you got?"

Channeling anger is just one more way of encouraging yourself to fight on, and Ernie was a master at it. He had the mindset that he'd go down fighting, no matter what the ocean threw at him.

From the very beginning of his ordeal, Ernie knew he had two options. He could give up and death would come quickly, ending his suffering. Or he could battle until every ounce of his energy was gone. Unlike Wardrop, Ernie did not have absolute faith that rescue would come. He simply kept an open mind that the final outcome could go either way, but he wasn't going to take the easy way out and help death along. Actively fighting for survival with positive affirmations was the path Ernie chose. He simply made up his mind he was not going to passively wait for death to take him. "I didn't spend all this time fighting," Ernie told himself near the end of three days of torment, "just to give up now. I'm going to pull this off." And he did.

When Ernie told himself "Good job, Hazard" over the smallest of achievements, I could not help but notice that this particular reinforcement was used by many other successful survivors. I call it *celebrating the little steps.*

In their 117 days adrift, Maurice and Maralyn Bailey reveled in small accomplishments, but also concocted days to celebrate. "Our female turtle was still alive, and we decided to keep her [to eat] to celebrate the following Sunday, exactly fourteen weeks since the *Auralyn* was sunk. I found it helped morale to have a day to look forward to and any event was made a celebration day." They celebrated birthdays, religious holidays, and anniversaries. "This way we always managed to be looking forward and not brooding over the past."

That last sentence is a key one, and every extreme survivor I've interviewed tried to do the same. That is why Loch kept telling himself "Be ready"—it was his way of looking forward. And Ernie never wasted a moment second-guessing himself or his crewmates when they were struggling to keep the *Fair Wind* afloat.

Viktor Frankl wrote about looking ahead in a Nazi concentration camp. He related how some prisoners, when working outside the camp, were given a token cigarette by a member of the construction company that was overseeing the project. That prisoner might later trade the cigarette to a guard or *kapo* for an extra scrap of food. But other prisoners who received the cigarette would smoke it as soon as they got back to the camp. Frankl observed that, if a prisoner smoked the cigarette they had received, they had given up. Rather than trading it for life-sustaining food, Frankl knew the prisoner instead wanted to enjoy one last smoke before dying. "Once they lost the will to live, they seldom returned."

Years ago, I had a conversation with Dodge Morgan, who completed the fastest solo circumnavigation of the earth by sailboat. I remember asking him about loneliness during his 150 days at sea, and he directed me to a chapter in his book, *The Voyage of America's Promise*. In it he wrote, "To cope [with being at sea for six months] I try to live life as short term as possible and to exaggerate and over-celebrate anything possible."

Dodge had his share of close calls, including numerous knockdowns and once being thrown overboard from his sailboat. Those brushes with death, combined with the isolation of the voyage, could have discouraged him from continuing. But, like the survivors in this book, he made a conscious effort to *seek out the positives* in his situation, no matter how small. [Ernie was thankful he had a can of water in his life raft, Loch felt fortunate to have a strobe light, and Wardrop, who had not a single supply or piece of equipment, was thankful for the turtle that visited him.]

Searching for something to be grateful for, or something to celebrate, goes hand in hand with pep talks; these simple actions help survivors maintain the willpower to fight on. No matter how bleak their outlook, they decide to *endure*. This does not mean that all extreme survivors are always optimistic. I consider Ernie's outlook during his ordeal neither too optimistic nor too pessimistic; instead I'd call him a realist, who didn't know if he'd be rescued, but was still determined to do his best. [*Doing one's best* is a phrase that Ernest Shackleton repeats multiple times in the journal he kept of his incredible ordeal in Antarctica, which we discuss in a later chapter.] Ernie believed he could influence his situation—by taking little steps and then congratulating himself—to help increase his odds of eventual rescue.

Other survivors are a bit different than Ernie, and they need to convince themselves that they will make it no matter what. In Al Santoli's book *To Bear Any Burden*, Dan Pitzer, a POW during the Vietnam War, stresses positive reinforcement: "When I think about all the guys that died in captivity and the guys that lived, it was a difference of just two words: *if* and *when*. A guy saying 'if I go home' is buried. But those who said 'when I go home,' or 'when I escape'— we survived."

Although individual survivors have different views on the degree of optimism necessary to survive, one aspect that is clearly detrimental is pinning one's hopes on salvation happening at a *particular time*. All too often, the survivors I've researched said that, when they fixated on a particular hour, day, or week when their ordeal would be over, they were devastated when it didn't come. The better strategy is simply to continue with the pep talks, little celebrations, and positive reinforcement for however long is necessary.

Survivors rely on "searching for the good," and we should too, for a healthier life. A study involving 97,000 healthy women ages fifty to seventy-four was conducted at the Pittsburg School of Medicine by Dr. Hilary Tindle. The subjects all filled out extensive questionnaires on their attitudes, and then eight years later, their health was checked. The women who expected good things to happen in the future had a 14 percent lower risk of dying in that time period than their pessimistic counterparts.

As important as positive expectations are, so too is self-compassion. In several studies conducted by Mark Leary, professor of psychology at Duke University, it was found that people who treat themselves with kindness, care, and encouragement are happier than those who give harsh self-criticism. Leary said that those people who treat themselves like a "kind friend" do best.

"When bad things happen to a friend, you wouldn't yell at him," explains Leary, and he encourages all of us to treat ourselves like we would a dear friend, with kindness and compassion. The survivors we examined in this chapter know this all too well. In their desperate hours, they found a variety of ways to pick themselves up, rather than sinking into criticism or berating themselves for their mistakes.

In our personal lives, we too often look to others for the uplifting pep talk or pat on the back. When I worked in the corporate world, I'd seek validation of my efforts from my managers. Others might be waiting for their spouse to acknowledge the long hours of toil devoted to a career. My advice is to throw that thinking out the window and be like the survivors we discussed. If you are involved in a difficult undertaking, give yourself the recognition you deserve, verbalize this positive feedback, and do so repeatedly. Don't wait for someone else to do it, because that day may never come. If you want to maintain motivation, it must come from within. Celebrate whenever you reach the smallest of milestones.

If your gut tells you that you are on the right track, stay with it. Don't seek the desired result within a specific time frame, but instead know it is coming and you are on the right track. Sometimes people give up because of a setback and miss out on a turn of events or lucky break that was coming their way. Prepare yourself to make the most of good things coming your way. How do you do that? "Lucky people create, notice, and act upon the chance opportunities in their lives," says Richard Wiseman, PhD, author of *The Luck Factor*. By being on the lookout for luck/opportunity, you increase your odds of getting it. For that to happen, you must be in the arena, rather than on the sidelines. In our day-to-day lives that means more participation, more experimentation, and more networking, but with extreme survivors it means staying alive, through positive thinking and actions, until the situation changes.

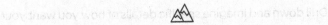

Some of my favorite quotes for enduring and maintaining motivation are shown below. I start with two very different entries from Shackleton's journal from when he and his men were trapped in Antarctica:

"We find the utmost difficulty in carrying through the day, and we can only go for two or three more days. We have done our best…"

—Ernest Shackleton

"I marvel at the sudden turn that leads from apparent certain disaster to comparative safety."

—Ernest Shackleton

"We should never despair, our situation before has been unpromising and has changed for the better, so I trust it will again. If new difficulties arise, we must only put forth new exertions."

—General George Washington to Major General Philip Schuyler concerning the loss of Fort Ticonderoga

"His decision to publish his work regardless of obstacles had inoculated him against depression."

—Richard Rhodes, referring to John James Audubon

## SURVIVOR LESSONS FOR YOUR LIFE:

- Douglas Waldrop visualized the details of his rescue to keep his spirits up and fight on. Visualization and manifestation should be in your arsenal of tools for attaining a specific goal.

Drill down and imagine specific details of how you want your goal to happen and how you will feel when it does. If thoughts of insurmountable hurdles pop up, simply picture yourself going *around* them and continuing to your destination.

- There is no denying luck plays a factor in so many aspects of life. But we can help attract that luck by taking steps to improve the odds of it happening and being prepared for when it comes. "Lucky people" have a secret: they have their antennae up and are looking for those little breaks and opportunities, and then they act on them.

- Practice positive reinforcement daily and say your encouraging statements out loud. Almost every extreme survivor in this book did that to come through victorious.

- Repetition of affirmations helps intensify your determination. And always keep an eye out for the humor and the absurdity of situations to break the tension.

- Plain old anger and resentment will get you nowhere, but *channeling* that anger into a positive fighting spirit like Ernie did is yet another way keep your spirits up. And if you can't think of how to channel it, use it for a great exercise workout! It's healthy and it clears the mind.

- Treat yourself the way you would a dear friend: with kindness and compassion instead of harsh self-criticism.

- For some reason, most of us are stingy about celebrating achievements. We are in such a rush we move right onto the next step without so much as giving ourselves a pat on the back. Ernie Hazard and Marilyn Baily taught me the importance of acknowledging the smallest of accomplishments to keep the momentum going. On the other hand, far too many of us are looking for a pat on the back from a spouse or a boss, and it never comes. Forget relying on someone else's affirmation. *You* should be the one to say to yourself "nice job." I no longer wait for really big accomplishments to rejoice; I find a reason to commend myself for smaller accomplishments, and I do it often—you should too. It gives a bounce to your step daily, no matter what life is throwing at you.

- Pinning your hopes that success or end of a problem will come on a *specific date* is a recipe for a let-down. Instead, just keep taking the little steps and celebrating small accomplishments; in this manner, you are immersed in the journey and know that you have done your part for the desired result.

- Remember how Dodge Morgan tempered his isolation during his solo circumnavigation of the globe: seek out the positives in your situation, no matter how small, over-celebrate any progress, then get back to work and repeat.

- All the talk today is about being in the "present," and that is certainly a good habit to strive for, but it is just as important to be forward-thinking. It's optimism that will keep you from brooding about the past. And, as Viktor Frankl pointed out, when under extreme duress, it can make the difference between who lives and who dies.

## CHAPTER 7

# RAPID RECOGNITION VS. DENIAL

"Tommy, when I woke up today I realized I had lost all compassion for these men. I don't hate them. But I'm ready to do whatever it takes to get out of here."

—Jason Smith

"I had his windpipe and kept yanking on it as hard as I could."

—Kevin McDonough

Some people freeze, some choose to ignore or pretend it's not happening, and others delay by over-analyzing. There are emergencies where any of these responses will lead to disaster, situations so grave that an immediate response is required. This was the scenario at the home of sixteen-year-old Shea McDonough and her parents, Kevin and Jeannie, on a hot, sticky night in July 2007. An intruder, Adam Leroy Lane, crept into their house through an unlocked door.

Shea was asleep in a guest bedroom to take advantage of an air conditioner and suddenly awoke when Lane's hand squeezed on her face, firmly covering her mouth and nose. "If you make any noise," said the intruder wearing a black ski mask, "I'll fucking kill you." He stood over Shea with a hunting knife and pulled the bed sheet down to her knees.

Shea thrashed, kicked, and tried to scream. Only a muffled cry came out, but it was enough to wake her parents in the adjacent bedroom. Kevin and Jeannie thought their daughter was having a bad dream and decided to check on her.

Many of us, especially at 4:00 a.m., would have paused and tried to process what we were seeing, had we been Shea's parents stepping inside the teenager's bedroom. Our minds, having never encountered anything like this, might have slowed down as we struggled to understand what was occurring. Then maybe we would have run for help, or shouted at the intruder. Instead, in a mere second, Kevin and Jeannie took the measure of what was happening—there was a hulking 5'11", 245-pound man with a knife on top of their daughter—and sprang into action.

Kevin, eighty-five pounds lighter than the intruder, leaped onto Lane's back and held his wrists. Jeannie immediately charged into the fray and tried to pry the knife out Lane's hand.

Lane was strong, however, and he managed to stand up with Kevin still on his back. If Kevin let go at this point, he would have certainly been killed, but instead he got an arm around Lane's neck and squeezed with all his might. "I had his windpipe and kept yanking on it as hard as I could," said Kevin.

Jeannie, still struggling to get the knife, had both her hands slashed, but she doggedly continued her efforts.

Incredibly, Kevin had the presence of mind to shout to his daughter. "Call 9-1-1 and get my gun!" Kevin did not have a gun, but "something inside me told me to say that which would keep him on his guard."

While the parents fought Lane, Shea picked up her cell phone and called the police.

Jeannie, despite her injuries, managed to wrestle the knife from Lane, while Kevin continued to squeeze on his neck. The fight went on for four minutes and suddenly a police officer ran into the room with gun drawn and hollered at Lane, "Don't move or I'll blow your head off!"

The arrest of Lane was fortuitous indeed: he had killed a woman in New Jersey just twenty-four hours earlier and prior to that had killed a woman in Pennsylvania. Kevin and Jeannie's heroic act surely saved not only their daughter, but other lives.

Lane was a truck driver from Jonesville, NC, and on the night he assaulted Shea he had parked his vehicle at a highway rest area, then walked a mile into town. He prowled around, peering through windows and checking for unlocked doors, before selecting the McDonoughs' house for the attack.

Consider all the other scenarios that could have happened had the McDonoughs froze or even hesitated for a few seconds. Had Shea not fought back, Lane would likely have raped her and possibly killed her. Had her parents not tackled the intruder, but instead shouted at him, Lane might have taken their daughter hostage. Given a few extra seconds to gather himself, it's also possible that Lane might have used his size advantage to kill first Kevin and then the two women. Instead, because of their rapid recognition of the severity of the situation coupled with the element of surprise, Kevin and Jeannie were able to control the psychopath until the police arrived.

Yes, it's possible that Lane might have exited the house after being confronted by the McDonoughs. But given his unbalanced state of mind and prior assaults, it's unlikely. It's also possible that Lane might have overpowered Kevin and Jeannie as they fought. We will never know. What we do know is that all three McDonoughs did their part to protect themselves and subdue this madman. Not one of them froze, not one of them hesitated, but instead immediately sized up the gravity of the situation and did whatever they had to do to fight off the intruder.

"What they did that night is unbelievable," said Chief James Murphy of the local police department. "Sometimes people freeze, but they reacted. With any hesitation, things would have turned out differently."

There are other emergencies where a survivor quickly recognizes the magnitude of the peril they are in, sees the need for bold, quick action, but has to wait for the just the right moment to make their move. That was the situation Jason Smith found himself in. There was no wavering, no denying the danger of his predicament, but instead he decided to do *whatever it took* to change the trajectory of events and keep himself alive. Like the McDonoughs, his was a judgment call that could be second-guessed, but it's clear to me he made the right decision because he acknowledged the severity of the situation.

Smith and fellow mountaineers Tommy Caldwell, Beth Rodden, and John Dickey were climbing a rock formation called the Yellow Wall, at 12,000 feet, in a remote section of Kyrgyzstan. On the morning of August 12, 2000, the climbers were sleeping in their two porta-ledges (suspended tents) hanging from a sheer rock cliff 1,000 feet up when a gunshot rang out, awakening them. A second shot was fired, hitting the cliff near the climbers as they tried to process what was happening. When the third bullet smacked the cliff so close to the climbers that it sprayed chips of granite on them, they knew the shots were meant for them. The four highly experienced American mountaineers looked at the slope below them and could see three men with guns, motioning that they should come down.

On the exposed ledge, the climbers had no cover, and no other viable option but to rappel down to the armed men below.

The gunmen were members of an Islamic militia, and it soon became clear that they planned to hold the Americans hostage for an unknown fate. Also held hostage was a Kyrgyz army soldier named Turat.

The captors forced their prisoners to start marching north toward Uzbekistan, approximately fifty miles away. Before the march, the rebels searched the Americans' base camp, taking the supplies they wanted, but gesturing to the Americans that they should keep their passports in their pockets. The climbers initially interpreted this as a positive sign, that they would be kept alive and traded for ransom.

As they began trudging northward, one of their guards left the group. Now only two rebels controlled the Americans and Turat.

On that first day of the ordeal, the rebels learned that Kyrgyz soldiers were approaching and they set up an ambush, careful first to split the hostages into two groups and keep them quiet at gunpoint. Using their AK-47s and a lone AK-74, the rebels killed two of the soldiers. Other soldiers returned fire. The terrified captives lay flat to the ground, hoping the burst of bullets missed them.

In the middle of the firefight, one of the rebels motioned for the prisoner named Turat to come with him. They ran behind a small hill and two reports from a pistol rang out.

Soon, the four Americans were moved to the same place Turat was taken and they saw his lifeless body, his head a bloody mess. Bullets from both the army and the rebels whizzed all around them and the climbers huddled together behind rocks for protection. At nightfall, the militia men moved their captives away from the army and then forced them into two tiny caves, with roofs no higher than eighteen inches and with cold, muddy floors. All four wondered if they would ever get out of the caves alive.

Smith thought their best chance of survival was to wait for the right moment and kill the guards. To do this, he first needed to gain the guards' trust. He began helping them in small ways and acted like he supported their cause. When the Americans were moved out of the caves—after seventeen hours of shivering—Smith assisted the rebels to maneuver a log across a river so they could cross. The rebels had struggled with the log and Smith went right into the raging rapids to finish the job, even as his captors shouted "Danger, danger!" Somehow Smith muscled the log to the opposite shore, impressing his guards and drawing approving nods from them.

Dickey, the first of the other three Americans to cross the log, asked Smith why he assisted the rebels. Smith replied, "We gotta get out of here." Dickey saw that Smith was indeed building trust, as one of the guerillas smiled at Smith and said, "You soljah?"

There was not a shred of doubt in Smith's decision, and no denial in his assessment that unless they took extreme action—the *do whatever it takes* approach—they would eventually wind up dead. Whenever he talked to the other Americans, Smith reiterated their need to kill their captors at the first opportunity. He was insistent that only they had the power to change the situation; no outside help would come, no Navy Seals swooping down to rescue them.

Subsisting on half a PowerBar per day and silty, brown river water, the four Americans were prodded on through mountainous terrain on August 14, 15, and 16, sleeping in confined caves or under boulders. Smith and Caldwell shared one hole, and Rodden and Dickey another. Smith relentlessly talked to Caldwell about different ways to overpower the two rebels, and slowly Caldwell came around to the same plan of action.

At one point Smith said, "Tommy, when I woke up today, I realized I had lost all compassion for these men. I don't hate them. But I'm ready to do whatever it takes to get out of here."

Caldwell nodded. He dreaded the idea of killing, but he agreed they likely wouldn't get out of the situation alive if they didn't act. He had seen the lifeless body of hostage Turat, and he knew the Americans could be next, especially if their captors felt slowed by herding the hostages around the mountains.

Caldwell also noticed that his stamina and strength were holding up better than the others, and if they were to overpower the guards, he would have to be involved.

Dickey agreed that escape by whatever means was their only option and that they needed to act soon. The lone dissenting voice was from Beth Rodden, who was prepared to spend months in captivity rather than resort to killing.

Smith continued to work on gaining the trust of the rebels. He was the first to tell his captors when he heard an army helicopter. And in difficult climbing spots he lent a hand to his captors, telling them they were good alpinists. The rebels slowly let their guard down thinking their prisoners compliant, and even helpful.

On August 17, one of the captors left the group to get more food, explaining he'd catch up with the group later. That left only one guard, a rebel that the other captors had called Su.

Later that day the group climbed a cliff with Su. Dickey, Smith, and Caldwell were aware this was their best chance to be rid of their tormentor. They needed to push Su off the cliff when his assault rifle was not pointed at them. But as Smith and Dickey awaited their opportunities, Su skirted both of them, out of reach.

The group was near the top of the cliff, and soon the opportunity would be gone. Caldwell realized it was now or never. Su was just above him. The mountaineer scrambled quickly but silently up to Su until he was just a couple feet away. Caldwell's foot dislodged a rock, and Su turned toward him.

Caldwell later wrote what happened: "Our eyes lock. I lunge for the strap of the gun slung around his chest. I pull as hard as I can and push his shoulder. His body arches backward through the blackness outlined by the moon. He cries out in surprise and fear. His body lands on a ledge with a sickening thud, and then bounces toward oblivion."

Caldwell sprinted to the top of the mountain. The stress of what he'd done gripped him and he curled into a ball and sobbed.

The other Americans briefly consoled him, telling him he had no other choice, and then they all ran diagonally downhill, eventually finding the Kyrgyz soldiers and freedom. [The rebel Su survived his fall and was imprisoned by the army. He was later tried and sentenced to death.]

The stories of the McDonough family and the mountaineers illustrate examples of bold action in life-or-death situations caused by other people intent on doing harm. In my opinion, both the family and the climbers had no other viable options except to fight their assailants to save their lives.

Other situations also call for an immediate assessment followed by drastic action, but do not involve a human adversary. That was the predicament Captain Chesley Sullenberger found himself in while piloting a commercial passenger flight out of LaGuardia Airport. His instant comprehension of a potentially deadly situation—loss of power in both engines when the aircraft hit a flock of Canada geese during its initial climb—is best related through Sullenberger's radio communications:

**Captain:** "Uh, what a beautiful view of the Hudson today."

**Copilot Jeffrey Skiles:** "Yeah. Flaps up please, after takeoff checklist."

**Captain:** "Flaps up. After takeoff checklist complete."

**Captain:** "Birds."

**Copilot:** "Whoa."

*Sound of thump/thuds followed by shuddering sound.*

**Copilot:** "Oh [expletive]."

**Captain:** "Oh yeah."

**Captain:** "Mayday, Mayday, Mayday. This is, uh, Cactus fifteen thirty-nine. Hit birds, we've lost thrust both engines. We're turning back toward LaGuardia."

**LaGuardia Air Traffic Control** *gives the go-ahead for a return and a half-minute later asks:* "Do you want to land on runway three?"

**Copilot:** "If three nineteen..."

**Captain:** "We're unable. We may end up in the Hudson."

In the next couple of seconds, the pilots and Air Traffic Control mention the possibility of landing at an airport in New Jersey. But forty seconds later, Captain Sullenberger realizes there was only one solution to get the plane out of the sky before it crashes.

**Captain:** "We're going to be in the Hudson."

**LaGuardia:** "I'm sorry, say again, Cactus?"

Captain Sullenberger and Copilot Skiles glided down toward the Hudson, ditching the aircraft in the river approximately three minutes after losing power. All 155 people on board safely evacuated the plane.

One can only guess what might have happened if Sullenberger, facing a situation he'd never encountered before, had hesitated before realizing he had to take decisive action.

In my research, the Sullenbergers, McDonoughs, and Smiths are the outliers. I've come across far more instances of denial and delay, and research by survival psychologists backs this up.

All too often, when a person experiences an extremely sudden and dangerous event, their initial reaction is denial. Maybe they think *This can't be happening to me*, or perhaps they minimize the risk and hope the trouble will soon pass. Either way, this often leads to precious time lost when they could have been seeking help or taking evasive action.

The chaos of a situation can also cause people to trick themselves into seeing patterns or connections that don't exist. Social psychologist Adam Galinsky conducted tests and experiments that showed that when people lack control, they often create a visceral need for order—even imaginary order. "When the world is uncertain, people grasp at straws," says Galinsky. He explains that, when chaos enters our lives, we become eager to push it away, and this can cause us to believe things that are not real.

Dr. John Leach, an expert on survival psychology, estimates that 80 percent of us will be stunned when a crisis occurs and that "reasoning is significantly impaired and that thinking is difficult." Many of the people in this category simply don't believe what they are seeing, which Leach refers to as the "incredulity response." This causes them to underestimate the seriousness of the danger.

Examples of this can be seen throughout history. At the beginning of WWII, the French military—despite their own reconnaissance to the contrary—were convinced the Germans would not cross the Meuse River without first digging in on the east bank and massing their artillery. The French also held to the belief that the Ardennes Forest was "impenetrable" to mechanized forces. Both were assumptions based in denial about the strength and boldness of the German army. [Maurice Gamelin, commander of the French, simply didn't believe in the "blitzkrieg" because he did not think it possible and because it didn't fit with long-held beliefs.]

When the *Titanic* collided with an iceberg, even after passengers were ordered on deck to prepare for boarding the lifeboats, many simply did not believe they were in any danger. After all, the ship was state-of-the-art, and sinking from their point of view was impossible.

More recently, the cruise ship *Costa Concordia*, steaming off the coast of Italy, was skippered by a captain stuck in denial as the ship was in serious trouble. Captain Schettino had deviated from the ship's standard course and hit rocks off Tuscany in the Mediterranean. At first, passengers were told "everything is under control, just an electrical problem," even as the ship was listing. [Whenever I hear "everything is under control," my bullshit antenna translates that message to "you'd better investigate on your own."] As the situation worsened, the captain was still hoping for a miracle: anything to avoid having to abandon ship.

Perhaps Captain Schettino's initial denial followed by a slow response was because the root of the disaster—this ship hitting the rocks—was of his own making: he was going too fast and too close to shore. Compounding his problem was the fact that, though the ship had been steaming for two days, he had not yet conducted the usual abandon-ship drill to instruct passengers on evacuating.

It was a passenger, not the captain, who recognized they were in extreme danger. She contacted a relative on shore and they in turn alerted the Italian Coast Guard, which immediately called the captain. Schettino, still in denial about the severity of the problem, did not ask for rescue, but instead requested tugboats. Only after the ship was listing perilously and clearly about to capsize did the captain give the abandon-ship order.

Then the captain and crew departed the ship while there were still 300 people aboard. Schettino later claimed he fell off the ship and landed in a lifeboat. There were thirty-two fatalities, but the number could have been 1,000 if wind had not blown the *Costa Concordia* toward shallow water. If the wind had blown the ship into deeper water, it would have sunk quickly, and rescue would have been much more difficult.

Denial comes in all shapes and sizes, and its genesis can sometimes spring from simply wishing things weren't so. We saw it in people refusing to leave New Orleans when Hurricane Katrina bore down on them. They thought the hurricane wouldn't be as bad as the forecasters were saying, and wanted to avoid the inconvenience of temporarily moving. A similar scenario played out during the COVID-19 pandemic, with people ignoring facts such as how hard the virus first hit New York City, and choosing to believe wearing masks was unnecessary, putting themselves and others in danger.

Others downplay the danger because of the delusion of personal invulnerability and the inability to adopt a new frame of reference. I believe this was the case with the captain of the tall ship *Bounty*, Robin Walbridge, during Hurricane Sandy. While not in outright denial, he was slow coming to the conclusion that his life and those of his crew were in extreme danger. In prior storms he had always come out on top, and perhaps that is why he downplayed the severity of the situation.

Walbridge never feared extreme weather. He was fond of saying, "There is no such thing as bad weather, just different weather." *Bounty* had weathered stormy seas and sailed around and trailed hurricanes before, and the captain saw no reason why he couldn't do so again. In a public access television interview conducted in Belfast, Maine, during the spring of 2012, Walbridge explained that he liked to "chase hurricanes" because his ship could get a good ride by staying behind the hurricane, taking advantage of the counterclockwise winds in the southeast quadrant. "When it [the hurricane] stops, you stop," explained the captain, "you don't want to get in front of it."

Ironically, getting in front of the hurricane was exactly what happened with *Bounty* in Hurricane Sandy as the storm moved northward off the eastern coast of the United States. Walbridge had initially steered a southeast course to pass the approaching hurricane on the east side. But Sandy was massive in size, and when *Bounty* was a couple hundred miles off the Carolinas, the captain realized he would have to go either due east—away from land and his destination of Florida—or try to rush to the southwest and sneak by the hurricane. He opted to change direction and head southwest, crossing in front of the oncoming storm, and try squeak by it on the landward side.

It was during this part of the passage that the ship's pumps began to fail. Waves twenty-five feet tall pounded the vessel, and the old wooden ship took on water faster than the pumps could expel it. This is when the captain—a bright and talented sailor—made his next fatal mistake. He should have called the Coast Guard—not a Mayday call, but an important call nevertheless, a simple report to tell the Coast Guard that *Bounty* was in the path of a hurricane and they were slowly taking on water. Together they could have worked out a game plan and established the needed periodic updates.

But Walbridge was in denial about just how serious the situation had become. Later that day, his first mate suggested it was time to let the Coast Guard know the *Bounty*'s condition and their exact position. Walbridge told him it was more important to focus their efforts on getting the machinery running.

The cloak of night closed in on the foundering ship, and this would add significantly to the danger, both to the sailors and to the potential rescuers.

Luckily, the first mate, on his own, used the satellite phone and alerted the ship's land-based trip coordinator that the vessel was without engine power and slowly taking on water. But because of a weak connection and shrieking winds, he wasn't able to clearly give complete details. The trip coordinator relayed what little information she had, and the Coast Guard instructed her to call the first mate back and have him activate the EPIRB so that they would at least know the exact location of the vessel. She relayed the message to the first mate and the emergency beacon was activated.

About an hour later, Walbridge acknowledged the problems were becoming dire, and he used email to give the trip coordinator more details. Still, the captain downplayed their predicament, writing, "We are taking on water. We are not in danger tonight, but if conditions don't improve on the boat, we will be in danger tomorrow. Let me know when you have contacted the Coast Guard so we can shut the EPIRB off. The boat is doing great but we can't de-water."

This message left the Coast Guard wondering just how serious the problem really was. Search and Rescue [SAR] Coordinators were in a conundrum: *If only we knew exactly what was happening on the ship. Why does the captain think they can make it to morning if they are taking on water in the middle of a hurricane? How can the boat be doing great if they can't de-water? Is he underestimating the seriousness of the situation?*

The answer to the last question was yes. But neither SAR nor the *Bounty*'s trip coordinator could communicate with the captain. The ship's electronics failed and only its hand-held radio, limited to a few miles, was working.

Thankfully, SAR and senior Coast Guard officials made the difficult decision to send a C-130 airplane into the storm to attempt radio contact. They would leave it up to the pilot to decide how close he could get to the ship's location, and to abort the mission if he felt he was putting his crew in extreme danger. Luckily, the C-130 did make it to the *Bounty*'s location. The aircraft and crew were circling overhead and looking through their night vision goggles when the ship suddenly capsized in the pitch black. Had the plane not been there, the rescue would have been delayed, and instead of saving fourteen of the sixteen-member crew, all might have perished. Captain Walbridge and Claudene Christian did not survive.

Walbridge may have been in denial, but he certainly wasn't frozen, the way so many of us react to a crisis. Some people literally become paralyzed, and it may not be through any fault of our own, but rather a biological factor. This reaction is seen in animals: when attacked, some animals play dead. The ploy sometimes works and the predator, seeing that the prey is no longer struggling, loses interest. I've seen this firsthand years ago when our cat brought home what I thought was a dead rabbit. I took the rabbit into the woods, dug a small grave, put the rabbit in, shoveled a scoop of dirt on it, and then got the surprise of my life. The rabbit hopped out of the hole and ran away.

Amanda Ripley, in her book *The Unthinkable*, interviewed evolutionary psychologist Gordon Gallup Jr. who confirmed this phenomenon: "Every animal [he tested] seemed to have a powerful instinct to utterly shut down under extreme fear."

This evolutionary trait may be one reason people freeze, but while it might work for a rabbit, it is almost always the wrong response in humans. Our emergencies are usually much more complicated than being attacked, and we need to rapidly process the information available. Our first step is to get through any initial denial and the physiological response of freezing. Then we need to do a quick analysis which should result in an answer to the question: *How much time do I estimate I have before I need to take drastic action?* If that answer is "plenty of time," delay can often be helpful, allowing you to analyze more options. But when the threat could overwhelm you in a matter of minutes, every second counts. You cannot afford to have "analysis paralysis" delay your response. Instead, be like the extreme survivors we discussed at the beginning of this chapter and adapt quickly to unfolding disaster, and be prepared *to do whatever it takes* to try and change the outcome in your favor.

And finally, when an issue involves mental health, don't wait for the problem to become critical—activate your personal "EPIRB" and ask friends, loved ones, or a professional for help.

# SURVIVOR LESSONS FOR YOUR LIFE:

- Rarely is a situation so serious, so dangerous that immediate—within a second or two—action is required. But should that happen to you, be decisive and act with the mindset to do whatever it takes to change the trajectory of the situation.

- When in peril, the first question you should try and answer is *How much time do I estimate I have before I need to take drastic action?* If that answer is "plenty of time," delay can often be helpful, allowing you to analyze more options. But when the threat could overwhelm you in a matter of minutes, every second counts.

- *This can't be happening to me* is called the "incredulity response" and is quite common, and it causes people to underestimate the threat. If you are in a perilous situation, recognize it for what it is and don't waste precious seconds delaying action.

- When you sense something is terribly wrong and you hear an authority say, "everything is under control," your bullshit antennae should be activated and you should start gathering as much information as you can to decide your next step.

- Finally, and perhaps most importantly, don't be like the *Bounty* captain and wait until you're in a personal "mayday" before letting someone know you are struggling.

## CHAPTER 8

# BLINDED BY THE GOAL

"Holy shit, this could be it! Another knockdown!"
—Bob Cummings

Bob Cummings [who we briefly met in an earlier chapter] had expended considerable time and energy preparing for his first Charleston-to-Bermuda sailing race. He had filled out all the necessary race forms, paid the entry fee, arranged time off from his duties as a Blackhawk helicopter pilot in the US Army, and over a period of several weeks had upgraded and modified his boat for the 777-nautical-mile voyage. He and first mate Jerry McCarthy had a brief window of time to sail the boat from its home port of Gloucester, Virginia, to Charleston, South Carolina, where the race would begin. They would have to leave on May 4 to make it to Charleston for the start of the race. Bob figured the relatively short two-day sail would allow him and Jerry to fine-tune their teamwork while giving the boat, named the *At Ease*, a good trial run and shakedown, affording the two sailors the opportunity to make any necessary adjustments before the start of the race.

The night before they set sail, Bob reviewed the marine weather forecast and realized that conditions were going to be nasty. A low-pressure system which had formed in the Gulf of Mexico was heading northeast, crossing over Florida, and was expected to then swirl northward along the eastern seaboard. Bob checked with one of his contacts at the National Weather Service and learned that he could expect seven-to ten-foot seas and winds up to thirty knots. In Bob's estimation, the weather would be borderline, pushing the limits of his forty-one-foot sailboat. He and Jerry had, however, previously sailed in similar conditions, and the two men had enjoyed an incredible ride on the *At Ease*. They handled seas up to twenty feet with a mixture of confidence and exhilaration.

That prior experience, coupled with the fact that they would miss the start of the race if they didn't leave as scheduled, led the two sailors to set sail as planned. Their goal of participating in the race was paramount.

Bob and Jerry enjoyed a bracing ride on the first day, with strong but manageable winds. During the night, the seas grew to eight to ten feet, but the men were in no jeopardy and the *At Ease* was performing quite well. Still, when morning came, the sailors reassessed their situation and digested the latest weather reports, which indicated they were in the peak of the storm and it would move past them over the next twenty-four hours. They talked things over and decided to push on. Bob did so after much deliberation; his twenty years as a helicopter pilot, including combat during Operation Desert Storm in Iraq, made him uniquely qualified to assess risk and his own capabilities.

The storm, however, intensified beyond the meteorologist's forecasts. It did so with such power that it took away the option of sailing into port. During the second night of their voyage, Thursday, May 5, 2005, waves grew from fifteen feet to thirty feet in just a couple hours, and gusts of wind reached an astonishing 100 miles per hour. Bob and Jerry handled the pressure-packed situation more calmly and rationally than 99 percent of us could ever do. They made all the right sailing moves and worked seamlessly as a team. But none of that mattered when a fifty-foot wall of water tossed *At Ease* upward and then sent it into a free fall.

When it landed in the trough of the wave the vessel's keel was topside and the mast was pointing down to the depths of the ocean. Bob and Jerry, tethered to the boat by their safety harnesses and now underwater, thought the boat would pull them both down with it. Bob started to unclip his tether's safety catch. His only thought was this: *Don't go down with the boat!*

Then a new thought—or maybe not a thought at all—made its case. Bob says a voice, which seemingly came from outside of his own mind, whispered to him, saying, *Bob, if you release from the boat you will die.*

Bob paused. Time seemed to stop. There was something about the voice, some confidence in its instruction, which made Bob take his hand away from the safety catch.

The vessel slowly righted itself, dragging Bob several feet behind like a fish on a line.

Jerry, however, had somehow managed to hold onto a railing and was still onboard the vessel. Together, they used every ounce of their strength to get Bob next to the boat, and then Jerry hauled him in.

The engine was dead. Below deck, the salon and galley were in shambles. Yet the overall integrity of the boat was in decent shape except for one blown-out porthole. The men screwed a piece of plywood over the porthole and tried to look past the mess in front of them. Both sailors, despite the trauma of being thrown into the sea, agreed that they were not quite in a Mayday situation yet.

Bob, being a helicopter pilot, didn't want to risk the lives of any aircraft pilots coming to his aid until he was absolutely sure the boat was going down. And so, he alerted the Coast Guard to their situation, promising to check back with them every half-hour. Then the two men sealed themselves in the cabin below deck to ride out the rest of the night.

But the storm was not done with them. Hours later, a rogue wave slammed into the boat, making the impact sound like an explosion. The vessel capsized again and the companionway hatch shattered. Water flooded inside the upside-down boat. Jerry thought, *Holy shit, this could be it! Another knockdown!* The men held their breath and prayed for it to come back up. When it did, they gasped for air, and watched more water cascade through the open companionway.

There was no question about it, they needed help. Bob issued a Mayday and activated the boat's EPIRB. A daring Coast Guard rescue ensued, and, after several agonizingly long hours when the sailor's lives were in the balance, Bob and Jerry were airlifted off the shattered boat and into the belly of a Coast Guard helicopter.

Years earlier, in 1985, on the other side of country at Yosemite's Half Dome, failure to give up the goal in the face of ominous weather resulted in an outcome far worse than that which befell Bob and Jerry. And in this instance, the victims had better information than the sailors had, along with a clear warning from hikers coming down from the mountaintop. But the lure of the summit proved too strong.

On July 27, 1985, five hikers began the grueling trek up the enormous monolith of rock known as Half Dome in Yosemite National Park. The upper portion of this mountain is sheer rock, with no trees and no shelter. It's not the kind of place you would want to be in a thunderstorm.

One of the group's leaders exchanged a few words with two young hikers coming down off the summit. The downhill climbers told the group not to continue onward, that there was the potential of a lightning storm hitting the mountain and it was much too dangerous to be caught on the summit.

Author Bob Madgic, in his book *Shattered Air*, chronicled the reaction of the upward climbing group leaders: "The warning sparked rather than doused Esteban's and Rice's motivation to pick up the pace." Esteban later described Rice this way: "When he committed himself to something it was all or nothing." In other words, he was blinded by the objective of reaching the mountaintop. Even when lightning flashed and thunder boomed, the hikers continued toward the summit, taking on Rice's attitude of *we've come this far, we're not going to quit now*. That mindset would cost two of the climbers their lives and leave three gravely injured when lightning hit the exposed summit.

One of the survivors, Bruce Weiner, later acknowledged he had put too much faith in Esteban and Rice because they had been hiking Half Dome for years. He warns others not to give in to group pressure if you feel otherwise, particularly if your intuition is making you feel uneasy. "One always needs to think for himself—in effect, not to relinquish control over his own destiny and allow someone else to determine it for him."

Weiner almost paid for deferring to the team leaders with his life. On the mountain, he had assumed that, because Rice and Esteban were veterans of climbing Half Dome, they could judge conditions better than himself. But being experienced doesn't automatically confer common sense or prudence. The two leaders of this group were ultra-competitive and equated caution with weakness. They were determined to a fault. The mountaintop was not far away when they were warned and heard the rumble of thunder, but they would not be deterred from their goal. They had planned the trip, packed for the trip, and now had put in several hours of hiking to get to summit. The possibility that electrically charged air might sweep over the Dome wasn't going to make them retreat. Retreating was for those with no heart, no courage, no commitment. Reaching the summit was the thing, and nothing would deter them.

That single-minded mission, with no adjustment to the plan of accomplishing it, was devastating to all five of the hikers. After the lightning subsided, another group of hikers arrived at the summit and found three of Esteban and Rice's group critically injured, another lying dead, and the fifth climber blown from the mountaintop by the lightning strike to his death below. If not for a heroic rescue by paramedics using a helicopter, the tragedy could have been even worse.

Whether the mountain is Half Dome, climbed by many, or Mount Everest, climbed by few, the goal can become so important it crowds out all other thoughts, especially when you've invested considerable time toward achieving that objective. But when new information is available, such as the deteriorating weather the Half Dome climbers were warned of, your objective might have to be delayed, altered, or put on the back burner until you can sort things out.

In the case of the climbers, the leaders ignored clear warning signs, while Bob and Jerry on the *At Ease* faced a much more difficult scenario to complicate their decision-making. The storm that hit them was much worse than the forecast, and it crept up on them in a gradual way until nightfall when it exploded. In the day prior to that, as the waves gradually increased, the sailors kept thinking they had seen the worst of things, and so they pushed on. Some of the hardest warnings to heed and reconcile with your goal are those that come on incrementally, subtly building. Bob's boat handled the increasing seas and wind quite well, and the men calculated that they could continue the voyage, mindful that if the weather became severe, they could head to the nearest port. But when the low-pressure system exploded in all its fury, the winds were too much for their sails, nor could they motor to safety because their engine quit in the rollover.

All of us, at one time or another, view a situation the same way Bob and Jerry did. Maybe we've spent months preparing, maybe we've juggled countless other obligations to make time for the trip, or maybe we've spent a small fortune toward whatever our goal is. It's not just sailors and mountaineers who get swept up in the moment and continue toward the prize. Ask yourself if you've ever said the words, "I've come this far, I might as well..." or "I've put so much time and money into this, I'm not going to back out now..." I know I have. We expend so much energy toward an objective, we become personally attached to it, allowing the objective to become a commitment. We trap ourselves because we don't want our prior efforts to be jettisoned, so we push on even when the path is littered with new obstacles, some of them potentially hazardous—perhaps dangerous to our health, dangerous to our finances, and dangerous to our families' well-being.

By turning the goal into a personal commitment, we lose some of our objectivity, because we then equate not following through with failure. But in reality, altering course has nothing to do with failure, but rather an unbiased look at more recent information that should give us pause. So banish the words "quitter" and "failure" from your journey toward your objective and replace them with "adaptable" and "flexible." Acknowledge that, when you made the plans, you didn't have access to new information. Be ready to strike out in a new direction or postpone reaching the objective.

One way to keep ourselves from being blinded by the goal is to ask ourselves what could go wrong. By doing so, we at least condition ourselves to be on the lookout for the pitfalls we've identified. Some of us will assess the new hazards and postpone the goal, modify it, or set a new one, while others may have a greater appetite for risk and decide the objective is so important it is worth the risk.

In his book *Dark Summit*, author Nick Heil relates the decision mountain climber Lincoln Hall made with regard to the risk and reward of scaling Mount Everest. In an earlier climb, Hall had made it tantalizingly close to the summit before nightfall and extreme cold caused him to turn back. A few years later, Hall came back to Everest and tried again. This time, the group he was with again came close to the summit, but decided to turn back to their uppermost base camp. Hall, however, just couldn't face the heartbreak of coming so close a second time and not reaching the top. "In the end," writes Nick Heil, "the risk of his own death didn't outweigh the overwhelming motivation for proceeding up—that otherwise he would have to go on living having once again fallen short of the summit."

Hall did make it to the top, but getting down was another matter. Suffering from altitude-induced cerebral edema (brain swelling), he could not make the descent and collapsed in the Death Zone, not far from the summit. Incredibly, he did not die, but was found barely alive by a climbing team the next morning. If not for the unprecedented efforts of Sherpa guides and fellow climbers who rescued Hall, his body would be forever frozen on the slopes of Everest.

Although Lincoln Hall lost the tips of some fingers and a toe to frostbite, he did recover and went on to write two books and enjoy life with his wife and sons in New South Wales, Australia. Sadly, he succumbed to cancer at age fifty-six.

Hall's appetite for risk in the name of the goal is actually quite common. Teddy Roosevelt's thinking was almost identical, when after his presidency he decided to explore an unknown river in the Amazon. Historian Candice Millard wrote in her book *River of Doubt* how Roosevelt told the president of the American Museum of Natural History that, if necessary, he was "quite ready" to leave his bones in South America. And that's almost what happened during his harrowing, months-long ordeal.

For people like Roosevelt and Hall—both infused with incredible inner fortitude and drive—no amount of new information would likely stop them from achieving a difficult objective. But for most of us, modifying our plans or goal makes perfect sense if new factors increase the potential for a bad outcome.

A slight twist on being blinded by the goal is something called the sunk-cost fallacy. This illogical reasoning causes us to continue to invest in a project even when the facts indicate the undertaking is not going to work. While most of the stories in this book involve physical survival, the sunk-cost fallacy can put an individual [or organization] in a financial survival situation. It happens when we think *I can't stop now, or all the money I've invested will be for naught.* That thought—really part of human nature to avoid a crushing loss—makes absolutely no sense. The money invested is gone. Now the decision should be this: do I cut my losses because the project is apparently not going to work, or do I throw even more money into the endeavor in hopes that it will all come together and the payoff will recoup my investment?

Only you can decide which is the right course, *but be aware* of the subconscious forces that can drive you to continue down the wrong path in hopes of vindication. The sunk-cost fallacy is much the same as the mountain climber who says "I've come this far, I just need to push on a little bit more for the summit"—even though the weather or another factor has taken a turn for the worse that will put you in jeopardy.

Sadly, this aspect of human nature also applies to friendships and romance. Many people put extra time into a relationship that clearly isn't working, simply because they've invested so much energy, time, and even love to keep it going.

I'm all too familiar with this thinking: I've done it on hikes, while boating, and with investments I knew little about. On one particular stock investment, where bad news within the industry made the stock go down, I made the mistake of "chasing a loss." The stock had dropped below the price at which I bought it, but I was reluctant to sell, hoping it would bounce back to my entry point, and only then would I sell. That way I could break even and feel somewhat vindicated. I was being loss-averse because I didn't want to accept the certain loss, but instead hoped [against reason] the stock would bounce back. And while I hoped and hung on, the stock kept tanking. Had I cut my losses by acknowledging the situation had changed [and with it my goal of making a profit], I would have salvaged some of the money invested. Instead, the company went bankrupt, and I received nothing. Simply put, I was blinded by the original goal and reluctant to face the new facts. And I'll bet if you think hard, you might have done the same, maybe not with a stock, but in regard to something you felt committed to, and *really wanted* to work.

It is easy to be blinded by the goal; the wisdom is recognizing when single-minded determination switches from being an asset to a liability.

## SURVIVOR LESSONS FOR YOUR LIFE:

- Deadlines are fine, but not for an activity that involves physical danger.

- If you ever catch yourself thinking, *I've come this far, I might as well keep going*, think again. Be aware that if you've invested time, money, and energy into the endeavor, you're likely to push on despite new information that should make you think twice.

- Not all goals should morph into personal commitments. It's okay if you don't reach the summit of your Mount Everest. There will be other, slightly different opportunities.

- It's easy to relinquish control to someone who claims to have more experience than you. But as soon as you feel they are out of touch with what is happening in the moment, don't be afraid to bail out.

- If you're involved in a threatening situation and you hear an inner (or outer) "voice," pay attention to it. This mysterious phenomenon has happened too many times to survivors in life-or-death situations to be dismissed.

- If you ever find yourself thinking, *I can't stop now or all the money I've invested will be for naught*, you are falling into the trap called the "sunk-cost fallacy." The money is already gone. Now you should take a step back and consider cutting your losses. Stay with the investment only if you feel the recent information you've studied means the situation will change for the better.

- Flexibility is the key when reaching for a goal. Don't hesitate to delay your plan or perhaps modify the objective when unexpected variables indicate the timing is not right. Too many of us are so focused on the objective, it's as if we have blinders on and miss the warning signs along the way.

## CHAPTER 9

# QUESTION THE EXPERTS (ESPECIALLY ON VACATION)

**"What? You've gotta be kidding me."**

Donald was itching to get out on the water. He and a group of friends had flown down to the Bahamas to bonefish, but high winds were limiting their fishing time. Donald was from Long Island and owned a boat there, using it to fish for bluefish, striped bass, and the assortment of other species found in his home waters. He especially loved time on the water because of the camaraderie with friends. Those friends joked that Donald was "Mr. Safety" because he was more prepared than a special operations force SEAL team. Donald took that as a compliment. He liked being prepared for any emergency, and he always heeded the weather reports before taking his boat out.

Bonefish don't live in the cold waters of Long Island, and Donald had recently been captivated by the idea of catching a bonefish on a fly rod in more southern climates. The sport held many components that appealed to him: maximum stealth and presentation were required, and he loved the fact that, when the bonefish were on the flats in shallow water, he could see his quarry. "What I care about," said Donald, "is that time seems to stand still when I'm fly-fishing, and I am consumed by the moment. The casting rhythm is relaxing and seeing the fish is extraordinary, prompting me to become a big fan of the sport."

But in the month of March, on one of the islands in the Bahamas, he was spending more time hanging out at the lodge than fishing because of the winds. When Donald and friends did get out on the water, it was difficult to spot fish, and even more difficult to make the pinpoint casts needed. Instead of the bright sunshine and gentle breezes they hoped for, each day brought slate-gray low-hanging clouds, wind, choppy water, and occasional cloudbursts of torrential rain.

Toward the end of his stay at the lodge, Donald and his friend Gene saw a break in the weather, and they agreed to be guided by a local man named Travis, who operated one of the lodge's flats fishing boats. The boat was a fifteen-foot Hells Bay with the gunwales about a foot off the water. These vessels are designed specifically for inshore flats fishing. Once the guide gets the boat on the flats, he shuts down the motor and climbs up to a poling platform at the stern of the vessel, both to better spot fish and to quietly pole the boat into casting range of the fish.

Travis motored the two anglers to a nearby spot, but the water was a cloudy with a light chop and the fishing was poor. Donald and Gene figured they would call it a day, understanding they had no control over the weather. Travis, however, started talking about his favorite fishing spot, and how its sand flats were in the calmer, less exposed lee of an island, and that they'd find plenty of bonefish there.

The only issue with Travis's special area was that it was a two-hour run in the small boat to get there, which neither Donald nor Gene knew at the time. But, with most fishermen, hope springs eternal, and they decided to give it shot. Travis knew the place like the back of his hand, and with his local knowledge, they hoped they would soon be fighting fish.

After a bumpy, uncomfortable ride to the destination, the men located schools of both bonefish and permit, and Donald managed to land a strong bonefish. Then rain began to fall, soaking the men and making visibility poor. It had already been a long day on the water, and the three men decided it was time to head for the lodge. They were cold and tired, but they were energized by the prospect of returning to the same fishing spot the next day.

It was now 4:00 p.m., and Donald thought it would be a good idea to let his friends and the lodge manager know that they would be running a little late and would be back around 6:00 p.m. He made the call, and then Travis opened up the throttle and the men started the long trip back. They took a pounding from the choppy seas, but Gene and Donald knew that once at the lodge, a hot shower, a drink, and dinner would make things right.

As the seas got a bit rougher, the nose of the boat, coming off a wave, was low enough that water came over the bow, flowing through the vessel and out the drain in the stern. Travis eased back on their speed. Then the skies and seas conspired to make the return trip even more miserable; the winds increased and torrents of rain pounded the tiny flats boat.

Each man was lost in his own thoughts as they gripped a seat or gunnel so as not to be tossed out of the boat. They just had to hang on, try to ignore the discomfort, and in Donald's case, say a prayer. He knew the situation was serious, but he had no idea just how dangerous the voyage would become.

About five minutes after Donald said his silent prayer, the drone of the engine suddenly ceased. The vessel had run out of gas.

"Where's the spare tank, Travis?" Donald shouted.

"I don't have one," said Travis.

"What? You've gotta be kidding me."

"No, mon."

Donald held his temper in check. Now was not the time to argue. The boat was drifting and taking on more water.

There was no anchor on the boat, but they rigged a grapple hook to an eight-foot length of polypropylene line. The line was too short and the grapple hook would not grab the bottom. Donald examined the ragged old polypropylene line and found a solution. The line had four strands, and he quickly uncoiled them into four sections, then tied them together in one very thin line of thirty-two feet in length. The men held their breath and dropped it over the bow, tied the end around a cleat, and were relieved when the vessel stopped drifting and its bow swung into the waves.

The men each put on a life jacket, with the best one going to Gene—as he did not know how to swim.

Donald and Gene looked at their cell phones, but there was no signal. The shivering men prepared to sit tight and wait for help to come. They used the coolers as a wind break. Water continued to come in over the sides and they took turns bailing with the Tupperware container that had held their lunch.

With daylight fading, they wondered how long it would be before the lodge manager realized they were overdue and a search could begin. It became clear to the men, with darkness falling, that they would not be found at night, and a search in the Bahamas is a bit different than in US waters: the Bahamas version of the Coast Guard, called BASRA, is a volunteer effort with limited resources. It would be a long wait before the volunteers could mount a search.

The castaways prepared for a bone-chilling night in the tiny vessel. They repeatedly tried to get a cell phone signal, but without any luck.

In the distance, they could see a beacon. After much deliberation, the men decided that, since the wind was blowing that way, their chances of rescue (and perhaps their very survival) would be better if they hauled anchor and drifted toward the land beacon.

The tactic was short-lived, as the boat quickly drifted parallel to the island rather than directly toward it and they had to drop the grappling hook again. As soon as the hook bit into the ocean's bottom, the boat swung around violently and a wave hit them broadside. Then disaster.

Within seconds, the stern was submerged. Suddenly the bow reared up and the three anglers were pitched into the sea as the vessel completely capsized.

The men instinctively swam to the boat and each one found a handhold on the overturned vessel to keep them together. Their chances of survival went from probable to maybe.

All three fishermen were already in the early stages of hypothermia. The cold ocean was sapping their strength as they clung to the overturned boat in the choppy seas. They tried not to think about sharks.

In the hours that followed, adrift in the darkness of an endless ocean, Donald prayed, thought of his family, and suffered from hallucinations induced by hypothermia and dehydration. The hypothermia was most worrisome at this point because one of the body's first responses to fight off the cold is to decrease blood flow to limbs. This helps keep the heart heated, but the decreased blood to the hands comes at a cost: it makes holding onto an object—in this case, the vessel—more difficult.

Donald also had plenty of time to consider how he got into this terrible ordeal. He knew the answer. It's a mistake I've made all too often, and so have many others.

Donald assumed that the local guide knew what he was doing. The guide took anglers fishing every week, so it would be logical to think that the vessel would be properly equipped and the guide would monitor their fuel. Neither turned out to be the case.

Making those assumptions almost got Donald and Gene killed. In the end he, Gene, and Travis all made it out of their nightmare at sea. When Donald's son, back at the lodge, realized his dad was overdue, he started working with Donald's brother to mount a search. They hired a private search and rescue plane to comb the waters in conjunction with a volunteer plane from the Bahamas. The men were finally located the next morning, hypothermic and in shock, but alive.

What could Donald have done differently? A short conversation with the guide before they left would have been helpful because Donald, being a boater himself, could have asked about safety equipment. He might also have taken a quick look around the boat before setting out. If he had done those two things, he would have learned there was no spare gas tank, no anchor, no working compass, and no safety devices onboard. He might also have realized there was no EPIRB or satellite phone that every boat the lodge worked with was supposed to have. These observations might or might not have caused him to abort the trip, but if he still decided to go, he might have thought, *It's not the best boat, so let's not go too far.*

Knowing Donald's adherence to safety on his own boat, he would have certainly thought, *This guide is playing fast and loose, I've got to monitor his decisions.* The guide may have been great at finding fish, but a discussion about the boat would have alerted Donald to the fact that safety wasn't the guide's top priority. But amid Donald's quest to catch fish and get the most out of a well-deserved vacation, this conversation never happened.

A similar incident happened to me when I accepted an offer to go striped bass fishing in Buzzard's Bay. I only knew the boat owner, Dave, from brief conversations on my neighborhood walk, and it never occurred to me to talk to him in advance about the trip—I was too focused and pumped with excitement about getting up the next morning and catching a giant bass. Dave, a friend of his, and I left at dawn in a thick fog.

Racing the boat along the shoreline, Dave was excited to get to his favorite fishing spot. It occurred to me he was going way too fast, but since it wasn't my boat, all I said was, "No rush."

About three minutes later, we heard a terrible bang and the boat shuddered. We had hit a rock. Dave slowed the boat and moved away from the shore. The vessel seemed to perform fine, so he decided everything was okay and continued to the rip we were going to fish, but at a slower pace. My warning antenna was now up, but I was already on the vessel, and I pushed out of my mind the thought of him aborting the trip and dropping me off at the dock.

When we reached the rip, it was rough as hell. The tide was going one way and the wind-driven waves came from the opposite direction, making for a chaotic chop. Standing up on the rocking boat to cast was dangerous. Adding to the difficulty: it started to pour, and more than one wave-top came into the vessel. I said, "This is unsafe, we ought to head in." Then the worst thing happened. His friend hooked into a nice-sized bass, and other bass were blitzing on baitfish all around us. "No way," said Dave's friend, "this is what we came for."

Understand that I live for that kind of fishing, and I've pushed the envelope many times when the fish are biting and the seas are rough, but one good thing about aging is it gives you wisdom. I bit my tongue for a few minutes. But then a wave came over the stern, where I was squatting down to change my tackle, and I was doused from head to toe. "That's it," I said. "Take me in and you guys can come back out."

I never fished with either man again. I did, however, get a call from the boat owner's insurance company. They said the boat had suffered $3,000 in damage to the engine and the hull and asked me to confirm the captain's story. I listened and said his explanation was correct and that speed was most definitely a factor.

My mistake that day was not only compounded by my desire to catch fish but also because I happened to be on vacation. Trust me, most of us, especially males, are so happy to be away from our jobs and other responsibilities that we let our guard down in pursuit of excitement and adventure. A vacationer has spent time and money to travel to do a certain thing, and they don't want anything to get in their way. It doesn't matter that we are new to an area and unfamiliar with local hazards; we just want to have a good time. And so we let our guard down.

One working vacation I took to Puerto Rico is a perfect case in point. I was there to speak to the Coast Guard Air Station about what I'd gleaned from survivors and accidents, when my own foolishness almost caused me to become an accident that would put Coast Guard rescuers in danger. I had a free day and went to snorkel at Hobos Beach. Giant waves were rolling in, but there is a long outcrop of rock curling out and back toward the beach like a fishhook that had relatively calm water on its inside edge. And just like Donald, I let the anticipation of the sport propel me forward, and I didn't even bother to ask a couple locals about the water: I was in vacation mode.

The snorkeling did not disappoint, and as I stayed along the sheltering rocks, the swimming felt nice and easy. And well it should—a current was taking me along. I hardly noticed the current because of the beauty of the colorful fish below me. (I had a mask and snorkel on, but no flippers.) Then, where the rocks ended at the open ocean, I decided to body surf some waves back, just like a couple of surfers nearby. That's when I noticed the current was exceedingly strong. A wave would propel me forward, but the backwash would take me right out again. After five minutes, I was making absolutely no progress toward land. I was being carried by the current parallel to the beach and by stroking hard I managed not to be taken further from the shore, but I was growing tired.

Had I been smart, I would have hollered to one of the surfers for help. But I was embarrassed to ask for assistance, and kept thinking, *Just one more minute and I'll be out of this current.* I didn't think I was in a rip tide, but I now started swimming more parallel to the shore instead of directly at it. After another five minutes, my feet touched bottom and I was able to rest on a sandbar. Then I swam for shore, and this time the current was still strong, only now it was taking me back toward the rocks where I first snorkeled. It was like being in a giant eddy.

I finally made it to shore, and as I lay panting on the sand, I counted all the many things I had done wrong. Perhaps the biggest mistake was that I entered unfamiliar waters when the ocean waves were enormous—*and most stupid of all*, I was all alone, and if I were dragged out to sea, no one would miss me. Wait, let me rephrase that: the Coast Guard, who had hired me to discuss decision-making by the smartest survivors and rescuers, would have realized something was amiss *the next day*, when I didn't show up for the presentation. By that time, I'd be halfway to Spain!

We get in trouble on vacation because we are relaxed, we're determined to have fun, we are in a new environment where we don't fully know the risks, and we cede control to local experts without monitoring what they are doing. The most frightening case that illustrates this is the vacationer from Florida who decided to go hang-gliding in tandem with an experienced pilot in Switzerland. Nothing wrong with that. [It's something I'd like to try even at my advanced age. It's not as if I need to have hours of training under my belt, because I'd be sharing the hang glider with the "pilot" who does all the flying.] The Floridian in this case did what all of us would do: put his faith in the pilot, who had years of experience.

And so vacationer Chris Gursky and the pilot ran off the cliff and into the wild blue. There was one little problem. The pilot had forgotten to fasten the vacationer's safety harness to the hang glider. In a terrifying YouTube video labeled "Swiss Mishap" posted by Gursky, you can watch how he grabs the pilot's safety harness to prevent himself from plunging over a thousand feet to the earth below. In mid-air, Gursky then uses one hand to grab the axle supporting the small wheels [used for landing] while keeping the other hand on the pilot. Keep in mind that they are flying at speeds of forty miles per hour and being buffeted by the wind. The pilot is aware of the situation, and he tries gripping different parts of Gursky's harness before finally getting a tenuous handhold on the front section. One of the most terrifying sequences is when Gursky's right hand loses its grip on the pilot's harness, and for a couple seconds he is only hanging on by his left hand. He eventually has to settle on gripping the pilot's pants leg.

The pilot steers as best he can for an open field. (If you watch this video, you will hold your breath wondering how long Gursky can maintain his handholds.) The two men come barreling toward the ground at forty miles per hour and, a few feet above the earth, Gursky loses his grip and smashes to the ground. Gursky is alive, but suffers a fractured wrist and torn bicep.

During that two-and-a-half-minute flight, Gursky never panicked and marshaled every ounce of strength to hang on. He displayed gallows humor when he posted the video, writing, "I will go hang-gliding again as I did not get to enjoy my first flight." And he wasn't kidding. He didn't want that experience to cause him to retreat into a shell, and a year later he was back in Switzerland, this time having a successful flight.

Like Donald, who never stopped fishing or going out to sea, Gursky showed courage and was not going to let one bad experience ruin his quest for adventure in the great outdoors. Nor did I stop snorkeling in new areas of the world; I just do a little research first, ask a question or two of the locals, and pay closer attention to the currents. And I'll bet on Gursky's second flight, he watched as the pilot clipped his harness to the aircraft, just as Donald will ask a future guide questions about the boat and the trip.

As for the pilot who forgot to clip Gursky's harness, he received a small fine for his oversight. A simple step will prevent other accidents like this from happening: a paper checklist before takeoff. On that checklist would be "fasten harness from guest to aircraft"! The pilot was deemed competent, but that competency was really never in question. The issue was *complacency*. Any expert can grow complacent simply because they have done the mission so many times successfully. The very act of doing one thing over and over can lead an expert to be lulled into shortcuts or forgetfulness. An activity, even as dangerous as hang gliding, can become routine, and it's human nature to move through the preparations quickly if all of your past missions have been successful. And that's what almost got Gursky killed. More on complacency, and its sister, overconfidence, to come.

## SURVIVOR LESSONS FOR YOUR LIFE:

- Don't assume local experts have taken proper safety measures. Sit down with that expert and review the plan and the safety equipment. Experts are no different than the rest of us: when we do an activity over and over, we must guard against complacency.

- It's natural to let your guard down on vacation in a new setting because you're determined to have fun. Remind yourself that you're unfamiliar with the local hazards, so ask lots of questions before enjoying your adventure.

- Donald, the fisherman visiting the Bahamas, showed good sense by not shouting at the guide when they ran out of fuel. When in a dangerous situation, don't fan the flames by assigning blame.

- Donald also illustrated "maximum use of all available resources" when he unraveled the four strands of the polypropylene line and tied those four together into one long line.

- If you ever find yourself, like I did, speaking to the Coast Guard about good decision-making, you might not want to almost become a SAR (search and rescue) case the day before you speak!

# CHAPTER 10

# DIGGING DEEP FOR OPTIONS & RESOURCEFULNESS

"[Metacom] spoke to me to make a shirt for his boy, which I did, for which he gave me a shilling. I offered the money to my mistress, but she bid me keep it, and with it I bought a piece of horse flesh."

—Mary Rowlandson

"Ah, Houston, we've had a problem."

—Jim Lovell

In an earlier chapter, we discussed emergencies where rapid recognition and response were essential. But what if the challenge is not as time-sensitive? Wouldn't taking the time to dig deep for more alternatives besides the obvious ones be helpful? If you believe options are the basis for sound decision-making, the answer is yes. The more options you consider, the better your chance of success. Extreme survivors ask themselves, *What am I missing and how can I view the situation from a new perspective? Is there a completely different way to solve the problem than what I've thought of?* Taking this extra step leads to ingenuity that was not readily apparent.

I've always thought I'd make a poor survivor because of my lack of technical and construction skills. If something breaks, particularly an item with moving parts such as an engine, I'm the last person you would want to fix it. I have difficulty understanding how the various components work together and struggle with pinpointing the source of the trouble. If I had to fix a broken solar water maker, as my friend Steve Callahan did during his seventy-six days adrift on a life raft, potential rescuers would have found only my bones.

I do possess an active imagination, however, so that if the problem before me is nontechnical, I've got a decent shot at coming up with a variety of options to either fix it or extricate myself from the situation. There is a quote from Marcel Proust I've long admired that gets at the heart of this kind of thinking: "The real voyage of discovery consists not in seeking new landscapes but in having new eyes." In other words, approach the challenge from a different angle, a different viewpoint.

One way to do this is to put yourself in another person's shoes. If you are waiting for rescue, imagine yourself as the rescuer. What would you be looking for? Where and when would you be looking? If your adversary is not the natural world (i.e., the ocean, extreme weather, etc.) but is another human, can you put yourself in their shoes? What can you do to make your situation more tolerable, more survivable? That is what Mary Rowlandson did in 1676, when she was taken captive by Native Americans during King Philip's Indian War. She is a perfect case study because after her ordeal she wrote an extensive account of her captivity.

Rowlandson was living in Lancaster, Massachusetts, when, on February 10, Native Americans raided her house, which also served as the local garrison. Forty-eight English settlers were either killed or taken captive that day. Mary was one of the captives, and her survival story spanned eleven weeks and five days of being held hostage in brutal winter conditions. Both she and her captors traveled across central Massachusetts and into southern Vermont and New Hampshire, marching through winter snows with little food, clothing, or shelter.

While other captives died along the route from starvation and exposure [many were dispatched with a "knock on the head" for complaining], Rowlandson endured. How did she do it? One of her most important techniques was to *consider every option*, particularly her skill at making herself useful to her captives and knowing when to speak up and when to suffer in silence. She also closely observed her captors and took note of how they managed to survive conditions almost as difficult as those she faced.

When her home was attacked, Mary and her youngest daughter Sarah were wounded. Mary had always thought it better to die at the hands of the Native Americans than be taken alive, but when the event actually happened, she reconsidered, writing "...if the Indians should come, I should choose rather to be killed by them than taken alive, but when it came to the trial, my mind changed: their glittering weapons so daunted my spirit that I chose rather to go along..."

For three days Mary, carrying her injured child, was marched west from Lancaster to the Nipmuc Village of Winnimesset. She was given no food and little water, arriving at the village exhausted and stiff from her wounds. But she took advantage of a lucky break when she met a captured English militiaman, who explained that when he was first taken hostage weeks earlier, the captors cured his wound with a compact of oak leaves. Mary tried the same technique and it cured her as well. Her daughter Sarah, however, was not as fortunate, and she died on the eighth day of captivity.

A few days later, another woman captive talked of trying to escape. But Rowlandson carefully considered her options and concluded escape would mean certain death from starvation and exposure, lost in the freezing wilderness. She wisely counseled against escape to her fellow captive, explaining they were thirty miles from any English settlement, and that in the dead of winter she would never make it in her feeble condition. This woman and her two-year-old child were later killed for complaining too much and begging to go home.

Rowlandson knew her best chance of survival would depend on acquiring enough food to stay alive, especially because the group of Native Americans and captives started on what Rowlandson called a series of "removes." These movements were a tactic used by the Native Americans both in their quest to find more food and to avoid direct engagements with Colonial militia. And so the group trudged westward again, where many an icy stream and river were forded. Food was so scarce they "boiled an old horse's leg, and so we drank of the broth as soon as they thought it was ready." She forced herself to eat just about anything she could choke down, including raw horse liver: "A savory bit it was to me: for the hungry soul every bitter thing is sweet."

Rowlandson had taken the extreme survivor's mindset *to do whatever it takes.* She would live with the help of the Bible she carried, the thought of seeing her husband and children [some were also held captive by different masters], and by a singular skill she had: knitting.

Refusing to be a passive victim, Rowlandson used every option available to secure food, letting it be known that she could knit or mend articles of clothing. Early in her captivity, she met Metacom, whom the English called King Philip, and he "spoke to me to make a shirt for his boy, which I did, for which he gave me a shilling. I offered the money to my mistress, but she bid me keep it, and with it I bought a piece of horse flesh." Rowlandson followed this up by making a cap for Metacom's son, and she was rewarded with a pancake made from wheat and bear grease. Word of Rowlandson's sewing and knitting talents got around, and soon she added stockings to her production of clothing, which she traded for a bite of food. And, like the mountaineers held captive in Kyrgyzstan, she was slowly gaining the trust of the Native Americans. She once received a knife for knitting a shirt and, instead of keeping the knife, presented it to her captor, "and I was not a little glad that I had anything that they would accept of and be pleased with." Hunger became so fierce, she described leaving a wigwam "to see what I could find, and walking among the trees I found six acorns and two chestnuts, which were some refreshment to me."

Shelter was also critical in the sub-freezing temperatures, and Rowlandson was usually able to sleep in her captor's wigwam. But some nights she was sent out in the cold and had to go from wigwam to wigwam until someone allowed her to stay. Surely, the fact that she was known to be useful because of her knitting played a role in her eventually finding shelter.

As the tortuous weeks continued, Rowlandson seemed to know when to speak up and when to keep quiet. At one point her mistress "told me I disgraced my master with begging, and if I did so any more they would knock me on the head. I told them they had as good do that as starve me to death."

Near the end of the eleventh week, Rowlandson learned that there was a possibility of her being ransomed back to her husband. Incredibly, the Native American leaders "called me to them to inquire how much my husband would give to redeem me." Her mind raced, because her very survival might depend upon the figure she recommended. Talk about pressure! "I thought if I should speak of but a little it would be slighted and hinder the matter: if a great sum, I knew not where it would be procured." She volunteered the sum of twenty pounds. A few days later, John Hoar, at great risk to his life, came to the encampment and secured the release of Rowlandson.

Consider that Rowlandson spent much of her eleven weeks of captivity slogging through snow while subsisting on a fraction of the calories in a normal diet. Her food intake would have been even lower had she not dug deep for resourcefulness and decided the Native Americans would treat her better if she made herself useful. She used many of the techniques we discussed earlier in the book, such as the power of little steps, thinking of others (her children), help from beyond (her strong religious faith), and the recognition that her situation was so dire she needed to have a "do whatever it takes" mindset. She also gained a measure of respect from her captors for her toughness and ingenuity.

What impressed me about Rowlandson's survival experience was the way she expanded her frame of reference from fixation on herself and broadened it to include her adversary, the Native Americans. Rather than give in to total despair, she pulled herself together and decided she did in fact have options in how to respond to her predicament. Escape was one option—the obvious one—that she reviewed, and then temporarily put aside. She knew she had been taken westward into the central part of the Massachusetts Bay Colony, a part of the region the Native Americans controlled. There were no nearby English settlements, and she rightly judged that if she fled into the woods, she would likely die from exposure and exhaustion.

Although starving with her captors, she did have some food, and was determined to get more. She was going to survive no matter what, and if it meant eating raw horse liver, that was what she would do. And to secure additional food, she ingratiated herself to her enemy. Note that, when she received a knife from a Native American for knitting an item of clothing, she decided not to keep it, but to give it to her "master." A knife, she decided, meant little compared to the goodwill she could earn by presenting it to the person who controlled her fate. It must have been a distasteful option to turn it over, but she realized access to food was the primary means of ultimate survival, and she wanted to have her captor think of her as useful rather than a complaining burden.

Rowlandson surely thought there might be a chance for escape at a later date, but to do that, she had to have some strength. And so, through making herself useful, she secured just enough food to live, and her fortunes changed when her captors decided to consider ransoming her. Like some of the other extreme survivors, she found a way to endure, knowing luck and opportunity might swing her way, and her job was to simply stay alive and be ready.

At the end of Rowlandson's account of her survival story, she shares these parting thoughts about life after captivity. "If trouble from smaller matters begin to arise in me, I have something at hand to check myself with, and say, 'why am I troubled?'... I have learned to look beyond present and smaller troubles and to be quieted under them. As Moses said, 'Stand still and see the salvation of the Lord.'" [Translation: I'll not worry about the little stuff again!]

Another compelling example of considering all available options is also from long ago, this one in Florida in 1528. It occurred when Spanish explorers walked through much of Florida searching for gold, and in the process missed the rendezvous with their ships. Leader and conquistador Cabeza de Vaca was responsible for getting his 250 starving men into this jam in an alien land, and now he had to find a way to lead them to salvation. Many were already perishing from disease and malnutrition.

Thinking that their best hope of survival was to build their own vessels and sail south toward Cuba (hopefully finding their mother ship on the way), the men had to use every bit of their ingenuity. None of them could have foretold that their ordeal would last eight years and only four would survive.

The Spanish had weapons and horses, but nothing to build a vessel with. The horses became their food, and the metal weapons were melted down to make nails and saws. Even metal stirrups and spurs went into their makeshift forge. For sails, they sewed their shirts together. Their vessels were nothing more than large rafts, and they used the tails and manes of their dead horses to hold the logs together. Cabeza de Vaca may not have been an effective leader, but he certainly was resourceful.

After the stranded explorers had consumed all their horses, they put their rafts in the ocean (just north of modern-day Tampa) and proceeded to cross the entire Gulf of Mexico in a deadly passage. One month at sea saw more of the men die, and by the time they reached the shores of Texas, their numbers had dwindled further. Winter in Texas claimed more lives from exposure and starvation, and the handful of survivors were held captive by the local Native Americans (the very people they came to conquer).

Cabeza de Vaca later recorded that only himself, two of his Spanish men, and an African slave named Estebanico were still alive after months of toil at the hands of their captors. These four used a creative method to stay alive: they convinced the Native Americans they had medicine-man powers. The men created religious ceremonies, loosely based on their Christianity, to show they had curative powers that their captors did not. They were also lucky. The Native Americans brought a man to them that they thought had just died, and the four strangers performed their cure and the dead man awakened. Cabeza de Vaca described how they treated sick Native Americans: "We made the sign of the cross over them and blew on them and recited Pater Noster and Ave Maria: and then we prayed as best we could to God our Lord to give them health and inspire them to give us good treatment."

While the Native Americans did treat them better, they were not free to go, and their captors sold them to other tribes. Historian Andrés Reséndez wrote "They were fed, protected, and passed off as though prized possessions from one indigenous group to the next. They became the first outsiders to behold what would become the American Southwest and northern Mexico..." Cabeza de Vaca and his three men eventually found themselves on the Pacific Coast, where a posse of Spanish slavers thought they were Native Americans and decided to capture them. Imagine their surprise when Cabeza de Vaca addressed them in Spanish! He and his men eventually made it back to Spain.

Cabeza de Vaca certainly fits the mold of extreme survivor in his use of limited resources to build the rafts from the tails of the horses, and to melt down the stirrups and convert them to nails. And once captured, he carefully observed his captors, just like Rowlandson, and found a need that he could meet. Rather than mending and creating clothing, he became a kind of "doctor," even if it was a sham. He used the very differences between him and his captors—language, appearance, religious ceremony—to his advantage, making his strangeness an asset in convincing the Native Americans that he could help heal the sick.

We now jump from centuries ago to more modern times to further illustrate how extreme survivors use ingenuity and resourcefulness to survive. Just as Cabeza de Vaca made the best of the few materials at hand rather than lamenting the absence of unavailable items, these modern-day survivors did something quite similar.

When astronauts have to use tape, cardboard, and socks to get from deep space back to Earth, you know someone has considered the full range of options. That was the case in 1970, when a short circuit caused an explosion on *Apollo 13*, destroying its oxygen tanks on the service module. Astronauts Jim Lovell, Jack Swigert, and Fred Haise were heading to the moon when they heard a loud bang, and minutes later Lovell looked out the window and saw "a gas of some sort" leaking into space. That's when the three men knew they were in real danger.

The command module, *Odyssey*, had just a little over ninety minutes of power and oxygen left. The astronauts were 295,000 miles away from Earth—a four-day journey.

NASA had not prepared for such an event because they hadn't thought the astronauts could survive such a cataclysmic failure. Mission Control and the three men trapped in space would have to figure things out on the fly. The astronauts quickly moved from the command module into the lunar module (the detachable craft that would normally be used for landing on the moon). Vacating the command module meant they could save its limited battery power for the return to Earth. But moving to the lunar module had its own issues: it was designed to support two men for two days, and now they needed it to keep three men alive for four days.

By brainstorming with Mission Control and digging deep into every option, the teams in space and on the ground performed a series of complex tasks to give themselves a shot at a landing on Earth. (If the accident had happened on their return voyage from the moon, none of them would have survived, because they would have already jettisoned the lunar module, which now became their lifeboat.)

Writer Tom Jones explained: "Their next struggle was against the cold. With most systems shut down, heat drained into the void outside." The temperature inside the lunar module dropped into the mid-thirties, making sleep over the next four days nearly impossible. Condensation caused their tiny space to drip with moisture, adding to the hardship.

Exhaustion and hypothermia, however, took a back seat to a new threat of asphyxiation because of an overwhelmed air-scrubber system in the lunar module. It seemed they were out of options. They had done their best, but replacing technological systems without the proper parts, tools, and supplies seemed impossible. Their salvation came in the form of instructions from Houston engineers to build a makeshift adapter. This is where the tape, cardboard, and socks were used.

As the hours and then days went by, it looked like they actually had a chance to reenter Earth's atmosphere safely. But they still had one big step to take: the astronauts had to crawl back into the control module and cut loose the lunar module. One of the concerns at this point was whether the condensation that had built up on all the wiring would short-circuit the reactivation of the command module. The process simply had to work. It did, and the crew survived, splashing down in the Pacific eighty-seven hours after the emergency began.

NASA and the astronauts credited their success to the hours of training. "The space program is built to handle problems," said Haise. That kind of training "helps you function normally even when you're aware of the serious situation you're in."

But all the training in the world means little if your core group involved with solving a problem doesn't consider every option and use every resource on hand, including socks and tape.

Inventiveness by astronauts and engineers in a team effort is something to admire, but I marvel more at the creativity of lone survivors, without another soul to bounce their ideas off. One story of survival that has stuck with me throughout the years is that of a motorist named John Vihtelic, who survived sixteen days trapped in his car. His accident occurred when his car veered off a mountain road and rolled several times, into a deep ravine more than 150 feet below the roadway. The twenty-eight-year-old had been driving through a remote section of the Cascade Mountains region in Washington State, a place where few motorists traveled. Those who did come by could not see his car far below.

Vihtelic could move his arms, but one of his legs was pinned by the crumpled car and a large root that had come through the windshield. Through the broken driver's-side window, the young man could see a swift-moving stream running just twelve feet away, so close but out of reach. He could last several days without food but not without water. The sound of the rushing stream mocked him. Vihtelic's shouts for help went unheard, and the horn on his car was broken. Survival was totally up to him, and the odds were not looking good. Situations like Vihtelic's have occurred before, and the car often stays hidden until a hunter comes along months or years later and finds a corpse inside.

Had I been in Vihtelic's shoes, the frustration of having the water so close might have made me crack. And I might have lamented that a crumpled car without a working horn would do me no good. Vihtelic, however, didn't waste a moment on self-pity, but instead took stock of the resources within reach, and his options to secure water. He thought of his car as a series of components and set to work dismantling the interior of the vehicle within reach. Also inside the car were a few personal items, such as a sleeping bag and tennis racquet. *Maximum use of all available resources* combined with considering every option would be his road to salvation.

Vihtelic tore the fabric off the car's ceiling and removed the long metal headliner strips that held the lining to the roof. He fashioned these into a "fishing pole" and made his "fishing line" from electrical wires removed from the car door and a cord from his sleeping bag. At the end of the line, he tied his T-shirt.

Next Vihtelic stuck the pole and line out the window and cast the T-shirt toward the stream. Eventually his casts became accurate enough that the T-shirt landed in the water. He let it soak a minute, then pulled it back into the car and squeezed the wet shirt, letting the droplets fall into his mouth. It didn't provide a lot of moisture, but by repeating the process, he quenched his thirst.

Later Vihtelic turned his attention to the root that pinned his lower leg and foot. Using a lug wrench, he whacked away at the root, but to no avail. Three days went by, and he fell into a routine of gathering water, praying, working to free his leg, and trying to keep his spirits up by reminding himself that he had to live so he could see his family again.

On the sixth day, he managed to remove the vanity mirror and secure it to the tennis racquet and reached outside, hoping the flash of sunlight that hit the mirror for a two-hour period in the afternoon would be seen by a passing motorist. For the next week he followed this routine, expecting that someone driving above would see him. When that didn't occur, Vihtelic knew he was so well hidden at the bottom of the embankment that no driver could spot him. If he was to live, he had to extricate himself from the car.

Jabbing at the root with the lug wrench had done little to cut through the fibrous wood, and each whack was causing him great pain. He knew that the wrench alone wouldn't do the job, and he needed something to hammer it with. Rocks lay outside on the ground, but none were close enough for him to reach. Fifteen days had gone by, and his strength was being sapped by lack of food and the cold nights.

Thinking of how he solved his need for water with the fishing rod and T-shirt, Vihtelic decided to try to scoop up a rock with the aid of a small leather suitcase and one of the rods from the car's ceiling. First, he bent the end of the rod into the shape of a hook. Next, he tossed the valise toward the rocks by the stream and then, using the rod, tried to scoop a stone into the open suitcase. It took him all day to finally nudge one into the valise. Shaking from the effort, he patiently put his hook through the suitcase's handle, pulled it back to the car window, and lifted it into the car. The rock was about the size of a softball, and it became his hammer.

Positioning the end of the lug wrench on the root, he struck it with the rock and saw that it bit into the fiber. Over and over, he chipped away, and was encouraged by the progress. But the headway came at a cost: as the root loosened, blood flow returned to his trapped foot, and the pain was excruciating.

Night closed in, and he forced himself to rest. He was hammering again at dawn, doing his best to ignore the pain. Then, three tortuous hours later, he shouted, "I'm free, I'm free!"

It took Vihtelic another hour to crawl up the slope, but he made it to the road, where he was found and rushed to a hospital. His foot had to be amputated, but he was alive, thanks to ingenuity and determination.

Resourcefulness comes naturally for a few of us, but for the rest, the trait can be learned. Stories like that of John Vihtelic's sixteen-day ordeal and his application of limited resources show us that even seemingly hopeless situations can often be solved with an open-minded approach to solutions that are not readily apparent. When you have time to carefully consider the problem—rather than a situation where immediate action is needed—don't pre-judge any option. Keep your mind open to everything. Creativity can percolate in your subconscious if you relax and don't rush. Sometimes the solution is right in front of you.

I recall reading about a man lost in the woods in the dead of winter and the despair he felt realizing he had no matches for a fire and knowing that building a lean-to would not be enough to ward off the icy wind. As the panic rose in him, he kicked at a fallen log in frustration. Bits of wood fell away where he had kicked. Rot had taken hold of the middle of the log. His salvation was at his feet. He kicked and clawed until he had hollowed out an area big enough to crawl into and lie down. Being out of the wind and in such a tight space allowed his body heat to be trapped in the wood and helped him survive.

The case studies in this chapter are very different from those in the Rapid Recognition chapter because the survivors discussed here had plenty of time to weigh options. In fact, the more options that are considered, the better. These extreme survivors kept asking themselves, *Are these the only options?* We should do the same: whether in a personal bind where nothing seems to work, or in a business setting before launching on a new path. Don't cede control to a narrow set of options, when so many more could be available by brainstorming or approaching the problem from a different angle. When I'm interviewing an extreme survivor, I often think that there are only two options, an "either/or" choice. But, as the survivor explains their account of action taken, I realize there are almost always more options than I had considered.

We can fall into the "either/or" trap when we let others frame the decision or issue. Many people (and managers) will say we can either choose x or y, and then everyone involved becomes fixated on only those two options, which are often either implementing a specific change or doing nothing. But in fact there are usually several alternatives to either going "all in" or keeping the status quo. Intermediate steps can be taken or practice runs can be implemented before a change is made, and perhaps several entirely different options should be considered besides the one proposed by the leader. In upcoming chapters, we will delve into this more, examining "groupthink" and reversible decisions.

Some of my favorite examples of looking at a problem from a new angle to arrive at a creative solution include:

- I once interviewed Naples, FL, police officer Jeffrey Perry of the Marine Unit, who described how a man's boat was hit by lightning, knocking out the engine and electronics in the Gulf of Mexico. The boater was uninjured but had no means of calling for help, and subsequently spent two weeks at sea. What likely saved him was his method to make sure he would drift back toward shore rather than deeper into the Gulf. He knew which way the mainland was by using his compass (or even the sun would have worked), but the breezes were variable and he wasn't sure about the currents. His solution was to throw bits of paper into the ocean. If the paper floated away from shore he would drop anchor, but if the paper moved toward shore, he'd let the boat drift in that direction. And by using the anchor in that manner, he eventually drifted close enough to shore to come within sight of other boaters.

- It's hard to believe this, but for many years the two-handed set shot, with feet on the ground, was the primary way outside shooters in basketball scored. Undersized player Kenny Sailors, in 1934, was getting his shots blocked, and started experimenting with jumping off the ground and shooting the ball with one hand. Suddenly no one was blocking his shot. "He was ahead of his time," *Sports Illustrated* reported. "When his first coach in the pros saw him shoot, he told Sailors, 'I need to teach you the proper two-handed set shot. That shot will never go in this league.'"

- In Florida, pythons sold as "pets" were released into the wild and now threaten dozens of native animals. Most people considered the problem insurmountable because it meant finding individual snakes dispersed in a vast wilderness. But one creative thinker came up with the idea of putting a GPS tag on an adult male python who will eventually "hook up" with a breeding female. You might ask how those who monitor the snake's movements know when it has found the female. Python hunter Tom Rahill explains: "Once they do locate the female, the distance they travel in a day will be severely reduced. They will kind of circle an area and that way the scientist will know that the male has found a female ready to breed." [One of the males released at the start of the program led the hunters to a 17-foot, 140-pound female with 73 eggs!]

- In 1913, Douglas Mawson led an Antarctic expedition that encountered disaster when one member of a three-man exploratory group crashed through a snow-covered crevice and fell to his death, along with his sled and sled dogs. Besides the loss of the explorer and the dogs, the sled was loaded with most of the food for the dogs and men, as well as their tent and other gear. The two survivors were five weeks away from help, with only a week and a half of rations. Soon the second member of the group died of exposure and starvation, leaving Mawson alone—with no dogs left to eat—still 100 miles from base camp. While trudging on alone, Mawson, with barely enough strength to walk, plunged through a snow bridge over a crevasse and was dangling at the end of the rope attached to his sledge above, which had luckily caught on the lip of the crevice. What saved him? Just days earlier, thinking such an accident possible, he had considered his limited resources and realized there was something he could do to give himself a fighting chance should he fall into a crevasse. He had tied a series of knots in his harness rope, affording a better handhold. Now, dangling over the abyss, Mawson put those knots to use. David Roberts, author of *Alone on the Ice*, describes how the explorer climbed to the surface. "He seized one of the knots, hung from it for a rest, then pulled himself violently upward until he could grab the next knot." When Mawson made it to the lip of the crevasse it collapsed and sent him plunging back down fourteen feet, until the rope jerked taut. Incredibly, hanging and twisting in space, Mawson gathered what little strength he had left and repeated the process, this time making it out of the crevasse. The simple innovative addition of tying knots in his harness rope saved his life, and eventually he made it to base camp.

So the next time serious trouble comes your way, think of the maximum use of all available resources—and those resources can be people you know or assets you may have overlooked. Banish the thought that you are out of options, and instead view the problem from a fresh perspective, asking yourself, *What options am I missing?* Don't decide on one until all possibilities have been considered. If an adversary has created your dilemma, view the issue from their perspective, and additional possibilities to improve your situation will surely arise. It worked for Mary Rowlandson, and it can work for you too.

## SURVIVOR LESSONS FOR YOUR LIFE:

- If you are in a situation that has a competitor (business or otherwise), expand your frame of reference to view the situation from their perspective. It may provide you with more options and a clearer strategy.

- Ask yourself, *What am I missing? How can I view this event from a new perspective?* The more options you consider, the better your chance of success.

- Refuse to be a passive victim. Think of Mary Rowlandson and her resourcefulness, staying productive until either an escape opportunity came along, or release.

- Training and practice may not cover the specific predicament you are in, but *Apollo 13* astronaut Fred Haise says it "helps you function normally even when you're aware of the serious situation you're in." Know your subject matter. Read, read, read, and contact those who have arrived at the goal you are aiming for.

- Maximum use of all available resources has put many survivors on the path to salvation. You can do the same on your path to your goal: for your resources, consider each and every one of your friends and acquaintances who might be able use their connections to propel you on your way.

- John Vihtelic's sixteen-day ordeal in his car shows us that seemingly hopeless situations often can be solved with an open-minded approach to solutions that are not readily apparent. Don't pre-judge any option.

- We can fall into the "either/or" trap when we let others frame the decision or issue. Many people (including managers) will say we can choose either x or y, and then everyone involved becomes fixated on only those two options, which are often either implementing a specific change or doing nothing. There are almost always more than two options available.

## CHAPTER 11

# EMOTION, ADRENALINE, AND THE ADVANTAGE OF PAUSING & REVERSIBILITY

"No matter how strong the urge, he tells himself, don't leave a moment before the water rises to the anchor roller."

—JP de Lutz

We've seen the importance of rapid recognition to overcome denial when immediate action is required. And we've examined how extreme survivors uncover every option and utilize all resources when time permits a more in-depth consideration of the problem. Now we analyze the implementation of decisions and responses, what traps to avoid and what techniques the toughest survivors utilized before putting a choice into action.

One lesson I've learned and put into practice after studying survivors for twenty-five years is to *choose the decision that is reversible* whenever possible. Good decision-makers don't like to be trapped, and they don't hesitate to make a U-turn and reverse a decision. They have deliberated on a number of options so that, when they select one, they are never reluctant to admit it was a mistake and can easily reverse course if they feel it increases their odds of reaching their objective.

This willingness to reverse course is the exact opposite of a pitfall that Rom Brafman, PhD, coauthor of the book *Sway*, describes as "diagnosis bias: our blindness to all evidence that contradicts our initial assessment of a person or situation." Being aware of this tendency can help us avoid it: there are almost always other options than the first one chosen. To keep those other options open, extreme survivors try to choose a decision that is reversible, so they don't get backed into a corner.

I've incorporated the preference for reversible decisions into my life. During my research for the survival story featured in my book *Fatal Forecast*, one of the survivors, who continued as a commercial fisherman, offered me a place on his offshore fishing boat to get a firsthand look at the work they do. I was quite interested, knowing this would help achieve a "you are there" feel for my writing about the incident, and so I asked the captain how long the trip would be. When he told me five days, I thought about the commitment. I'd never been 200 miles out to sea on a relatively small boat, and I knew that if I went on the trip, they weren't going to head back to shore if I became seasick. If you have ever been seasick, you know there is truth in the saying, "When you first get seasick you think you're going to die, and as the sickness goes on, you wish you would die!"

Simply put, I did not want to be trapped on a boat for five days, yet I also felt the experience would be beneficial. I was torn about whether or not to go. I thought of some of the survivors I'd grown close to over the years, and decided to do what they would have done—go with the reversible decision. I told the captain I'd pass for now but was interested in working on a commercial boat for a day trip and then later, if I felt I needed to be at sea for a week, I'd join his crew.

The day trip I went on involved exhausting work, and I realized I had made the right choice by turning down the longer trip. The decision allowed me to achieve a feel for the labor of a commercial fisherman without being confined on a small boat for a long period of time.

I've also found the maxim *avoid getting trapped* useful in day-to-day life. It was handy when I coached young, inexperienced basketball players. Oftentimes, when a child had the ball, he would dribble down the sideline and then an opposing player or players would seal him in the corner. My player's only option at that point was to make a difficult pass. I explained to my team that it's best to keep more options open and go where you have choices. I encouraged my players to stay out of the corner (I called it Death Valley), and instead dribble up center court to the three-point line. From there all sorts of options would be available: they could drive in for a lay-up, take the outside shot, or pass to the open man.

The "avoid dribbling into corners" analogy—choosing a reversible decision whenever possible—has served me well in many instances. For extreme survivors, those practices helped save their lives.

Equally important is keeping emotions in check when making big decisions. How do we do this? If the situation allows a period for reflection, extreme survivors simply let time pass before implementing a decision. That way, the power of the emotion has dissipated and they are able to approach the situation rationally, rather than in a cloud of emotion, which can generate impulsive reactions. (Think of impulse as something only a teenager would act on, and counter it by whatever means works for you, from deep breaths to calling a friend for advice.)

It's important to be cognizant that adrenaline gives us energy, but has a downside as well. Quite often fear, or anger-induced emotion, can cause us to have tunnel vision. "By virtue of its fear response," writes Marc Schoen, author of *Your Survival Instinct is Killing You*, "the limbic brain (our more primitive portion of the brain) has now commandeered the ship and is reacting and making decisions based on fear, while drowning out the invaluable input of the rational, cerebral brain."

Adrenaline triggers the fight-or-flight response. Those two options were fine throughout most of humanity's time here on Earth—such as what to do when a saber-tooth tiger is approaching. But in the modern world, with its complex problems [other than an urgent physical threat], fight-or-flight-type choices are much too limiting. We know that the more options we consider, the better the chance of selecting the correct one. Yet the physiological effects of adrenaline make complex thinking difficult because so many chemicals are flooding the body with one purpose: immediate action.

When we feel threatened or experience extreme anger, our hypothalamus/sympathetic nervous system sends signals to our adrenal glands, which secretes adrenaline and norepinephrine into our bloodstream. Our blood pressure goes up, and so does our heart rate. This is followed by the discharge of cortisol, which in turn releases glucose to give us that fast-acting extra energy for the upcoming fight-or-flight. In essence, our body is screaming, "Do something!"

Unfortunately, the deluge of chemicals interferes with the neural pathways to our prefrontal cortex, which we use to analyze options. Diane Hamilton, a mediator and contributor to the Harvard Business Review, gives a clear explanation of what happens when prefrontal cortex activity is diminished: "Complex decision-making disappears, as does our access to multiple perspectives. As our attention narrows, we find ourselves trapped in one perspective." She explains that in essence we're filled with a flashing red light indicating danger, prompting us to react, protect, attack! This is certainly beneficial for the people in the life-threatening situations outlined in the chapter on Rapid Recognition, but harmful in more complex circumstances where we have several minutes, hours, or days to respond. Thoughtful, rational processing of information is what is needed with most problems, but the adrenaline rush so overwhelms us that we lose our situational awareness and our ability to think through different possibilities because all our focus is on the one thing that caused the reaction, without benefit of the larger picture.

Sometimes it's impossible to avoid the surge of pure emotion which prompts an adrenaline release, but you can avoid *acting* on it by simply letting time pass. The old advice to "wait twenty-four hours" or "sleep on it" before making an important decision are beneficial rules to follow. Given a situation where you know how much time you have before you must make a decision, delay is a wonderful antidote to an emotion- or adrenaline-induced response.

One of the best illustrations of these decision-making tips involves President John F. Kennedy during the Cuban Missile Crisis. Faced with potential nuclear war, he was certainly in a survival situation, albeit quite different than the examples in the previous chapters. Kennedy was literally faced with the survival or fate of the world, and you can't get more pressure-packed than that. I became deeply intrigued by how JFK conducted his decision-making process while cowriting a book about the actions of the President and the U-2 spy plane pilots during the Cuban Missile Crisis. Because Kennedy secretly audio-recorded every meeting he had with his advisors during the crisis, it is the perfect case study to analyze how decisions were made...and changed. What follows is an inside look at the flow of the President's thought process.

President Kennedy was still in his pajamas on the morning of October 16, 1962, when there was a knock at the door. National Security Advisor Mac Bundy had urgent business with the President. In Bundy's hands were photos shot by a U-2 spy plane over Cuba that showed Soviet medium-range ballistic missiles capable of carrying nuclear warheads.

The President remained calm and quickly chose his team of advisors, calling them together for the first of many meetings at 11:45 a.m. [The advisors were called the Executive Committee of the National Security Council, or ExComm.] Before the meeting even started, Bobby Kennedy was shown the intelligence photos, and in contrast to his brother, he erupted in fury, saying, "Oh shit! Shit! Shit! Those sons-of-bitches Russians!"

Perhaps the difference in the two brother's responses was that the President had been in a wartime survival situation and Bobby had not. JFK had been on a patrol torpedo boat, a PT-109, when a Japanese destroyer plowed into it at night during WWII. He'd seen death firsthand, and he had also experienced that surge of adrenaline and learned to channel it toward a goal that would save both himself and his crew. Kennedy had experienced how adrenaline has its place, providing focused energy, but he also recognized the need for calm, calculating, deliberative thought when making critical decisions. The PT-109 survival ordeal helped him greatly during the Cuban Missile Crisis.

When the first ExComm meeting commenced, the head of the CIA's National Photographic Interpretation Center, Art Lundahl, and another expert, Sydney Graybeal, showed the group three enlarged black-and-white photos of a missile site in San Cristobal, Cuba. The President asked two strategic questions—quite similar to what the very best extreme survivors we have reviewed would have done. The first was to establish that the threat was real so that no one could be in denial, and the second involved establishing a time frame for when action would be needed.

**President Kennedy:** How do you know those are missiles?

**Lundahl:** By the length, sir.

**President Kennedy:** Is it ready to be fired?

**Graybeal:** No, sir.

**President Kennedy:** How long?...We can't tell that, can we, how long before it can be fired?

**Graybeal:** No, sir. [Later that day the President was given an estimate that the missiles would be operational in approximately ten to fourteen days, which turned out to be accurate.]

When the President learned when the missile could be fired, it gave him a rough deadline to work with—he didn't have to make a decision on how to remove the missiles immediately. This certainly proved advantageous, because the emotions of the group during that initial meeting were supercharged: the Russians had secretly placed missiles in Cuba while publicly stating that no offensive weapons would be deployed to the island. Consequently, the majority of the advisors [a mix of military and political appointees] favored an immediate military strike to remove the missiles while the US had the element of surprise.

President Kennedy leaned toward this solution as well, but to his credit, he had the group *consider all options*. There was never any doubt in the President's mind that the missiles had to go, but he wasn't ready to commit on exactly how that would be achieved. At the end of that initial meeting, it's important to note that he did not authorize the massive airstrikes the group discussed. Such a decision would have been irreversible—once implemented, it would have ruled out any diplomatic or intermediate steps. Instead, the President wanted *more* information.

**Bundy:** Mr. President, we have a decision for additional intelligence reconnaissance [from the U-2 spy planes].

**President Kennedy:** We'll go ahead with this maximum, whatever is needed from these flights.

And so, within day one of the crisis, JFK utilized many of the survival lessons we have discussed: he demonstrated a rapid recognition that the emergency was real, followed by establishing a rough time frame for when he would have to act, put all options on the table, sought additional information and intelligence, and finally resisted the pressure, at least temporarily, to initiate a decision that would be irreversible.

That pressure to act increased by the hour. When the same group reconvened that evening, General Maxwell Taylor, Chairman of the Joint Chiefs of Staff, had an exchange with the President in which Taylor pressed for a full-scale air attack immediately, before the Soviets learned that the missiles had been discovered by the US. Taylor drove this point home by basically saying the option of a limited air strike was abhorrent to the Chiefs and the action had to be total annihilation of all military targets in Cuba.

**Taylor:** Mr. President, I should say that the Chiefs and the commanders feel so strongly about the dangers inherent in the limited air strike that they would prefer taking no military action rather than to take that limited first strike. They feel that it's opening up the United States to attacks which they can't prevent if we don't take advantage of surprise.

**President Kennedy:** Yeah, but I think the only thing is, the chances of it becoming a much broader struggle are increased as you step up the [attacks].

The President at this early stage was still strongly leaning toward an air strike, but as the hours went by and his emotions dissipated, he began to seriously consider other options. After all, if nuclear war was the result of his actions, millions of souls might perish—it was crucial to methodically examine the possible repercussions of any decision.

In the days to come, the military leaders continued to press the President to attack. But JFK was now leaning toward a blockade of Soviet ships headed to Cuba. General Curtis LeMay, Air Force Chief of Staff and head of Strategic Air Command, upon learning that Kennedy was considering a blockade rather than a surprise full-scale bombing of the island by air, was furious and on the edge of insubordination.

**LeMay:** This blockade and political action, I see leading into war. I don't see any other solution. It will lead right into war. This is almost as bad as the appeasement of Munich.

*Comparing Kennedy's potential action with Neville Chamberlain's notorious appeasement of Adolf Hitler was quite an insult. But LeMay wasn't done.*

**LeMay:** I think the blockade and political talk would be considered by a lot of our friends and neutrals as being a pretty weak response to this. And I'm sure a lot of our citizens would feel that way too. You're in a pretty bad fix, Mr. President.

**Kennedy:** Re-say it?

**LeMay:** You're in a pretty bad fix.

*Instead of exploding,* **Kennedy** *simply responded: You're in it with me.*

The President was not going to be rushed or pressured by anyone. He bitterly remembered how he had failed in his decision regarding the Bay of Pigs. Kennedy had not asked the military leaders enough questions, nor did he have them submit various alternatives, and he agreed with their time frame. The President had a bad gut feeling about the mission, and instead of aborting it, he made it a certain failure, watering down the invasion by reducing American aircraft involvement. Now, with the Cuban Missile Crisis, he pressed the military to submit a variety of options. This time he would listen to his gut feeling, and that was telling him he needed more information and must not be rushed.

Ultimately, the President used a variety of tools—the blockade, diplomatic pressure at the United Nations, communication with Soviet Premier Khrushchev, and bargaining chips [US missiles in Turkey]— before he would commit to massive airstrikes on Cuba. He never ruled that out, but he considered it a final step, not a first step. [See Appendix for the fourteen steps JFK took to assist his decision-making during the crisis.]

With the facts at our disposal today, as well as hindsight and declassified CIA documents, we know that had Kennedy attacked Cuba, it likely would have started WWIII, with nuclear weapons. And even with his steady leadership, few people realize just how close we came to nuclear war on a day known as Black Saturday, October 27, when a number of unforeseen incidents had us a whisker away from Armageddon. One of the incidents involved the Russians shooting down a US U-2 spy plane over Cuba, killing the pilot. The President had earlier assured General LeMay that, if the Soviets shot down of one of our reconnaissance planes, LeMay could send in his fighter jets and take out the surface-to-air missile site. Yet when that very event happened, Kennedy reversed himself and did not allow LeMay to attack. Instead, he gave Bobby Kennedy an instruction to offer the Soviet Foreign Minister one last deal, with the implied threat that, if the offer was not accepted, military action was imminent. Had JFK stuck with his original assurance to LeMay, this single event could have been the trigger that started all-out war.

When I think of JFK and the Cuban Missile Crisis, I'm reminded of another leader who tamped down his emotion by pausing, which some historians might call delay. General George Washington arrived outside Boston in July 1775, when the Minutemen had the British surrounded in the city. His initial thought was to attack: the enemy was trapped and he thought the moment was right. Washington convened his war council of subordinates, many of whom were from the Boston area, and he was surprised when they advised him to wait. They had seen the severe losses the British took at Bunker Hill when they attacked an entrenched enemy, and they knew how costly a ground assault on Boston could be. Washington decided that he could delay. He *listened* to the overwhelming sentiments of the subordinates that were from the area, and chose the path that was reversible, deciding to continue the siege with the option of attacking at a later date. In the meantime, he would gather more intelligence.

There was one more crucial reason General Washington could afford to delay: Henry Knox was on his way with cannons taken from Fort Ticonderoga. Knox's progress was slow, but he was making headway. When the artillery finally arrived, Washington had it placed at the Dorchester Heights, looking down at the city and the harbor. British General Howe realized Washington had outmaneuvered him— the Patriots could hit both British troops and their supply line, which was the ships. Howe had no choice but to evacuate Boston, and he sent word to Washington that, if he was allowed to leave untouched, he would not destroy the city. And so, the British boarded their ships and sailed to Nova Scotia. Washington took control of Boston without any attack or loss of life, his objective achieved simply because he tamped down his impulse and emotions and knew time was on his side.

Kennedy and Washington had days, not hours, to put emotion aside, move away from their initial inclination, and let their rational mind take control. Our next crisis and individual, Jean Pierre (JP) de Lutz, had only minutes to do the same.

JP and I developed a friendship when I was researching his survival story and became intrigued by one particular decision he made in a pressure-packed situation. It was one of those moments of self-control I knew I'd never be able to achieve, nor, I believe, would most of us. I wanted to learn the full story, and how he managed to stay calm in chaos. One of the answers was that overruling adrenaline-induced action can be learned.

JP's story begins on his sailboat, the *Sean Seamour II*, on a voyage from Florida to France in May of 2007. Onboard were JP, Rudy Snell, and Ben Tye. A few days into the voyage, they were ambushed by subtropical storm Andrea approximately 240 miles off Cape Hatteras, North Carolina, and 400 miles from Bermuda. Meteorologists would later call it a bombogenesis storm because it formed and exploded so rapidly.

With no ports nearby, the three sailors were at the mercy of the powerful seas. The vessel was performing well. All sails were down, and a drogue was deployed to slow their roller coaster ride down the waves. The men had sealed themselves in the belly of the boat to ride out the storm.

It was nighttime, approximately 1:00 a.m., when they heard a thunderous boom. Then their world turned upside down. A rogue wave, much bigger than the preceding waves that had been hammering the boat, sent the men careening through the cabin like pinballs as the vessel was knocked on its side, masts underwater. The boat righted itself quickly, the sailors shaken but unhurt. JP began to head topside to check damage. As he climbed the companionway steps, he calmed himself. *Think everything through. Nothing rash.*

JP had been in a knockdown before on a solo trans-Atlantic crossing, and the experience was so terrifying, he had considered activating his EPIRB, the emergency beacon. Instead, he assessed the damage to the boat and decided the vessel could withstand the thirty-foot seas a bit longer. He had to endure a night of constant battering and frayed nerves, but when morning came, the wind eased slightly. Now, in subtropical storm Andrea, he hoped for a similar outcome.

With a safety harness on and its tether clipped to the vessel, JP slid back the companionway hatch and was immediately assaulted by stinging spray. He squinted and was surprised to see that the deck light still shone. But there was damage indeed: the entire hardtop dodger had been ripped away and the upper part of the helm pulpit cracked off. A million thoughts raced through JP's mind, but paramount was the safety of his two crewmates. *We've had a capsizing and we are hundreds of miles from help. What will happen if an even bigger wave hits the boat?*

JP decided he must activate the EPIRB, so the Coast Guard would know their position and assist them as soon as C-130 aircraft and helicopter pilots could safely launch. Once back inside the vessel, JP explained his decision to turn on the emergency beacon, and his two companions agreed, Ben thinking if they got hit by another rogue wave it could be too late to call for help, and Rudy concerned about injury to one of the crew should another knockdown happen.

The men hunkered down to wait for dawn, hoping the wind would decrease. But the storm had other ideas. At approximately 3:00 a.m., the sailors were engulfed by another monster wave. The boat began its sickening roll, and when it passed the forty-five-degree mark, fear shot through JP. Caught inside the vortex of the colossal wave in what seemed like slow motion, the vessel was turned completely upside down. [Marine experts and Coast Guard pilots later estimate the largest waves were in excess of eighty feet in height!]

Green seawater came flooding into the vessel, and JP was trapped under the top of the salon table, which had come free of its legs. For a moment it seemed he would drown inside his own boat long before it sank. Every neuron and nerve in his body was firing as adrenaline coursed through his limbs, but he could not move. His shouts for help, however, were heard by Ben and Rudy, who lifted the table off JP.

Two feet of water were sloshing around inside the overturned vessel, and more was slowly coming in through the ceiling vents, which were now on the floor. JP had suffered seven broken ribs, but the adrenaline helped him ignore the pain as he dove down into the water to the companionway to exit the vessel. His one thought was to see if the life raft was still with the boat—he knew they were going to need it. As he swam out of the overturned vessel, it suddenly started to right itself, and within seconds JP found himself on the floor of the cockpit. Taking in deep gulps of air he noticed the eerie quiet when the vessel was in the trough of the waves and the shrieking wind when it rode to the summits.

The mast of the *Sean Seamour II* had cracked off, and JP's eyes widened when he saw the inflated life raft stuck under the fallen mast at the side of the boat. He managed to free the raft, but in the process the mast broke more of his ribs. JP realized the raft's canopy and ballast bags had to be torn off in order to free it. Here, the power of adrenaline gave JP the strength he needed to do the work while also overriding the pain in his chest.

After securing the raft tightly to the vessel, he descended the companionway back into the cabin where Ben and Rudy were bailing water furiously. The two sailors waited for JP to tell them if the life raft was still with the vessel—they were ready to board. Here is when JP made the decision few of us could. *We've got to stay with the boat. We can't leave until I know she is sinking.* He repeated this warning to himself, and then addressed his crewmates: "The life raft is secured to the boat, but its canopy is gone and so are its ballast bags. We need to stay with the boat as long as we can."

This is one tough decision to carry through on. Imagine you are entombed in a cabin where the water is gradually rising and your fear-induced adrenaline is screaming at you to GET OUT! Most of us would do just that, afraid the boat could start sinking at any moment. But JP forced himself not to act on that feeling. Instead, he listened to his rational mind, which told him there would likely be more time before the boat sank, and the sailors would be far safer with the boat than in the damaged raft, being battered by rampaging seas.

JP, clutching his chest, looked toward the front of the vessel. He estimated that, when the water inside the boat reached the anchor roller, it would be time to get out. *No matter how strong the urge,* he told himself, *don't leave a moment before the water rises to the anchor roller.* He knew how difficult it would be to board the life raft at night and hoped that the *Sean Seamour II* could stay afloat to daybreak.

He wasn't so lucky. Two big waves crashed into the boat at 5:00 a.m., sending it careening down the face of the waves. Green water poured in through the companionway hatch, which had broken. The water rose beyond the anchor roller.

JP staggered up the steps, and in the dim light he could see that the bow of his beloved vessel was partly underwater. "It's time to go!" he shouted down to his crewmates.

Thanks to a heroic rescue by a Coast Guard helicopter crew, JP, Rudy, and Ben lived to describe their ordeal. Sadly, a nearby vessel, the *Flying Colours*, with four young men and women onboard, disappeared without a trace.

Earlier I said I doubt I could do what JP did, and part of that comes from looking at my own response to adrenaline. Even when your mind knows the right thing to do, it's damn hard to follow logic when you're flooded with adrenaline. That's what happened to me while fishing on a river in northern New Hampshire. I decided to cut through some high weeds and brush because that section of the river was deeper than the tops of my hip waders. Suddenly, not more than ten feet in front of me, the brush shook and I heard a deep-throated huff. Up sprang a black bear! The wind must have been blowing from him to me, because I believe this bear never got a whiff of me or heard me until I was just a few feet away. But it sure saw me now. I'd read all about what to do when encountering a bear—don't run, or you will trigger the bear's chase instinct (not much different from how a dog would react). The proper action is to slowly move away, preferably sideways. Let me tell you that is not what my body, particularly my legs, was signaling to me. Every neuron in my body was on full alert and seemed to be screaming at me, *RUN!* That was the rush of chemicals, the fight-or-flight response, and with a 300-pound bear in front of you, it's difficult to ignore the "flight" part of that signal.

It took all my inner willpower to ignore that impulse to run. Instead, I froze for three or four seconds, pupils dilated, heart racing, body tensed. Then slowly I took one step back, then another, always keeping my eyes on the bear. The bear did something similar, moving away, but painfully slowly.

You might have had similar experiences. If you've ever been caught in a rip current at the beach, you know the right thing to do is to take your time and swim parallel to shore, and you will eventually be outside the current. We know that's the solution, but when you are being dragged out to sea, the fear-induced adrenaline isn't telling you to do anything slowly. It's saying *Get to safety, NOW!* And if your rational mind isn't in control, the supercharged fear you feel might compel you to try to swim all-out via the shortest route back to land, not parallel to shore.

The trick is to size up the situation and determine whether you have time to pause to give your rational brain a chance to regain control of what action to take.

We have learned to recognize that two very different responses are called for, depending upon the time sensitivity of the event. If your daughter is being attacked, like what happened to the McDonoughs in a prior chapter, that's clearly an immediate action situation, where adrenaline is welcome. It gives you strength to fight. But far more common are situations where we have the comparative luxury of knowing we have a few seconds or longer to take action. In these circumstances, pause and allow the adrenaline to recede a bit, so that you can move from your reptilian brain to your thoughtful, calculating one. Acknowledge the extreme emotion you are experiencing by saying, "Here's what I'm feeling, *but I don't have to act on it right now...*" Think of all the scenarios you will solve coherently, from road rage to heated disagreements with a loved one, to bumping into a bear in the woods. Instead of going with a half-baked impulse, quiet yourself down and ask yourself, *What would a wise man or woman do?* It may not be the knee-jerk reaction you initially thought of.

I close with one personal story that will sound quite familiar to many of you. Years ago, when I worked for a corporation, I received an email from a colleague that I interpreted as snarky, condescending, and rude. Two other managers had been copied on the email. My fingers went right to the keyboard and I clicked on "Reply-All," then started typing a response that was just as pointed and edgy. But before I hit "Send," I recalled a similar incident where this coworker and I had gotten into a "pissing match," which ultimately made us both look bad. Now, with my emotions running high, I wanted to respond immediately and not give my coworker additional minutes of smug satisfaction before I turned the tables on him. It sure was difficult to pause and not click "Send." But I talked to myself, saying something like, *Calm down, you're mad as hell, you can reply tomorrow.* That made me put the email in a draft folder and wait until the next day to decide whether to send it.

Well, a funny thing happened the next day. Somehow, the email from my coworker the previous day seemed to have a different tone. It didn't seem condescending, but more like a gentle push to get me to consider adding his idea to the technical paper I was writing. While I wouldn't have used the same language or approach he had, the email no longer looked like a personal attack. It's amazing how that one email went through a metamorphosis in just one night.

Go with the decision that is reversible, pause if you can, and remember adrenaline has its pros and cons.

## SURVIVOR LESSONS FOR YOUR LIFE:

- Beware of "diagnosis bias," where we hold onto our initial assessment even when evidence contradicts it.

- When an incident causes you to feel emotion building, and you don't have to respond right away, let time pass until the emotion dissipates. And if the situation causes an adrenaline burst, be aware that it can trigger the fight-or-flight response. Again, the solution is to let time pass so you can calmly consider a host of responses beyond fight-or-flight. "Sleep on it" doesn't mean worry about the event at night, but instead lets you calm down for a more measured response the next day.

- Another way to curb anger or surging emotion is to pause and say to yourself, "Here's what I'm feeling, *but I don't have to act on it right now...*" Once you have calmed down, ask yourself, *What would a wise man or woman do in this situation?*

- Next time you feel pressured to make a decision, be like JFK and refuse to be rushed by the Curtis LeMays of the world.

- When given the option, chose the decision that is reversible.

## CHAPTER 12

# FOR AS LONG AS IT TAKES

"This was the bitterest blow of all and people just gave up after that. Four days later there were only nine of us left."

—Tony Large

## EXPECTATIONS, TIME FRAMES, TAKING THE LONG VIEW, AND CALMING OTHERS

Nineteen-year-old Tony Large was involved in one of the most unusual and tragic events of WWII, often referred to as the "Laconia Incident." His recounting of his ordeal—only four out of fifty-one men survived many days in a drifting lifeboat—has much to teach us about expectations.

Tony may have survived because he kept his emotions in check whenever rescue looked imminent. He did not pin his survival on a specific incident or time, but instead was determined to fight for *however long it was necessary to make it out alive*. Incredibly, this young man had this wisdom during the Laconia Incident because it was not his first time in a life-or-death situation at sea.

The *Laconia* was a British ocean liner converted to troop ship during WWII, and was traveling from South Africa to Plymouth, England, with over 3,000 souls onboard. The passengers were a mixture of military, a few women and children, Italian POWs, and their Polish guards. On September 12, 1942, the *Laconia* fell into the crosshairs of U-boat Commander Werner Hartenstein.

Torpedoes sank the ship, and Hartenstein heard cries for help
in Italian, prompting him to realize there must be Italian POWs on
it. Wanting to rescue his allies, he asked U-boat headquarters if he
could try and do so, explaining he didn't have time to sort out who
was Italian and who was not. He received permission to declare
the area a neutral rescue operation on open radio airwaves. The
commander had a large red cross painted on a white bedsheet,
which was placed on the surfaced U-boat, and then he proceeded
with the rescue. With the help of two other U-boats, the Germans
started retrieving survivors regardless of nationality.

Tony Large, a young man from Great Britain, was in a lifeboat. It
was one of many the U-boats gathered up on a tow line to keep them
from drifting off until a ship could arrive and take all onboard. This
was the second time Tony had been on a ship sunk during the war.

While his lifeboat was being towed by the U-boat, an American
aircraft inexplicably attacked the U-boat, even though the
Americans knew a rescue of British troops and passengers was
underway. One of the American bombs landed just ten feet from
Tony's lifeboat, blasting him into the water. He managed to crawl
back into the boat; many others were not as fortunate and drowned,
or were attacked by sharks. The U-boat men, of course, cut the lines
to the lifeboats, and then took the sub beneath the sea's surface
for safety.

Tony and fifty-one other men crowded into the lifeboat and
spent the next thirty-nine days adrift with little food or water. They
were 700 miles from land, with just three gallons of drinking water.
His survival account is told brilliantly in his book *In Deep and
Troubled Water,* as well as in a letter he wrote to his parents four
days after his rescue. The survivors, he explained, occasionally
caught fish using a bent nail as a hook. Their thirst was so great
they drank the fish blood and sucked on the eyeballs for moisture.
For some, the lack of water was too much to overcome, and several

castaways gave in to the temptation to sip seawater. Tony and twenty-nine others resisted the urge and were alive on day 17.

When I read the book and Tony's letter, the incident that occurred on day 17 really captured my attention. It involved a freighter that passed just 300 yards from the lifeboat. "We could not believe her lookouts would fail to see us, or fail to hear our screams and our yells..." But that is exactly what happened. "This was the bitterest blow of all and people just gave up after that. Four days later there were only nine of us left." He recounted that the despair was just too much for many of the survivors, that their expectation to be rescued by the ship—only to have it steam right past them— prompted many to start drinking seawater. Talking about a friend and fellow survivor, Tony wrote, "I was not observant enough, or trained enough, to calculate the depths of his misery or his sense of hopelessness after the unhappy passage of the north-bound cargo ship." His friend calmly climbed over the side of the lifeboat and paddled away to his death. Such was the effect of the near-rescue.

Perhaps Tony endured because of his prior brush with death, and he knew that help can come at any time, you just have to fight on as long as you can. Those who gave up only needed to hang on three more days—that's when it rained and the life-giving moisture kept Tony and three others alive for a few more days. [Despite the rain, five of the nine people still alive died from their weakened condition.] On the thirty-ninth day, Tony and one other survivor saw another ship approaching. The two remaining survivors were asleep. "We didn't dare wake the two sleeping forward because of the general depression it would cause if the ship did pass us by." Only when he was sure the sailors on the ship had seen him did he wake the men. The two castaways who had been asleep would not sit up or even bother to look, but instead said, "Don't joke about things like that."

But this was not a cruel joke, and all four survivors were saved, having drifted over 600 miles. In Tony's letter to his parents, he said the thing that kept him going was "the thought that after you two had sacrificed and done so much to bring me up and launch me, I should waste your efforts by drinking salt water or taking a walk [suicide]."

Like many of our other extreme survivors, Tony cites fighting to live for loved ones as a reason to carry on. Equally important, however, is that Tony had learned from his prior experience adrift that salvation comes on its own time, and the job of the survivor is to wait it out. Tony knew that he had a clear option to end his suffering by drinking seawater like so many others did, but instead he rallied from the blow of the ship that steamed right by him. His decision reminded me of Ernie Hazard, adrift in a life raft, who explained how he knew he could end his suffering at any time by simply giving up, but had decided to go down fighting. It was not an easy resolution. "Giving up was an attractive option," Ernie said, "and I did everything I could not to dwell on it or think too much about going down that path. I knew the odds of being found were long, but I was going to see it through."

Tony, like Ernie, had learned not to put a time limit on salvation, but rather keep fighting until it came. They never stopped believing rescue was possible, but they didn't pin all their hopes on a specific time frame for it to happen. For the rest of us, when faced with adversity or striving toward a difficult goal, the trick is to stay as even-keeled as possible, despite setbacks and delays. Although near-misses can feel crushing, keep the hope that the next chance at rescue—or reaching your goal—is coming.

United States Senator John McCain offered a variation on this mindset when he wrote about his experience as a POW in North Vietnam from 1967 to 1973. McCain was a Navy pilot, and his ordeal began in October of 1967, as his dive bomber was rocketing at an airspeed of 500 knots over Hanoi and was hit by a Russian-made missile. The aircraft went into a spin, plunging toward the earth, and McCain pulled the ejection handle. The force of the violent ejection caused both arms and his right leg to break, and the thirty-one-year-old pilot lost consciousness. When McCain came to, he was in a lake, and local villagers pulled him out and started beating and kicking him.

The North Vietnamese then took him to the main prison in Hanoi and told him they would withhold medical attention until he gave them more than his name, rank, and serial number. McCain stayed silent. He was eventually taken to a hospital, after the North Vietnamese learned his father was an admiral. The hospital treatment was little better than the prison, and McCain's weight dropped from its normal 155 to 100 pounds. After six weeks, he was brought back to prison and put in a cell with two other pilots. McCain was in rough shape and could not even sit up, but his fellow pilots attended his needs. "They were allowed to get a bucket of water and wash me off occasionally," said McCain. "They fed me and took fine care of me, and I recovered very rapidly."

The luxury of having cellmates only lasted until March of 1968, and for the next two years, McCain was held in solitary confinement. This was a different kind of trauma than his physical injuries, but no less a torture. "As far as this business of solitary confinement goes," wrote McCain, "the most important thing for survival is communication with someone, even if it's only a wave or a wink, a tap on the wall, or to have a guy put his thumb up. It makes all the difference."

The North Vietnamese actually offered to set McCain free, thinking world public opinion would improve if they changed how they treated prisoners. But McCain was not going to allow himself to be used as a prop just because his father was an admiral. When he rejected his interrogators' offer, he was asked why. McCain explained, "I said that Alvarez [first American captured] should go first, then enlisted men and that kind of stuff." His interrogators were enraged and told him, "Now, McCain, it will be very bad for you." And one and a half months later, that's just what happened. He was taken to a small room and bound with ropes. "For punishment they would almost always take you to another room where you didn't have a mosquito net or a bed or any clothes. For the next four days, I was beaten every two to three hours by different guards. My left arm was broken again and my ribs were cracked."

As the months and years dragged on, McCain did his best to survive. He wasn't allowed books, so in his mind he reviewed those he had read, and he continued to tap on the walls in code to fellow prisoners, getting beaten when he was caught. He found that prayer helped, especially asking for guidance to do the right thing. But the one lasting takeaway when I read his memoir was his opinion that a survivor must take the long view and not get their hopes up on rumors of release or a peace deal. "We had a saying in prison: 'Steady strain.' The point of the remark was to keep a close watch on our emotions, not to let them rise and fall with circumstances that were out of our control." He explained that some prisoners got their hopes up over something as small as finding a carrot in their soup, thinking the guards were fattening them up before release. Then the next day, when there was nothing extra in the food, their spirits would sink and they would become despondent. "Prison was enough of a strain without riding an emotional roller coaster of our own creation."

When McCain saw a prisoner taking a short view of his life and predicament, he would remind them of the steady strain philosophy. "It was best to take the long view. We would get home when we got home."

Taking the long view means continuing to survive. And it can have a calming effect. Even for those lost in the woods, such thoughts can be the difference between life and death. The terror of being lost—and I've been there—makes you want to move quickly as nightfall approaches. But unless you really know the way out, you are far better off spending the night in the woods, rather than groping around in the dark where you could break a leg or fall off a cliff. And if you have told someone where you were going and when you expected to return, eventually help will find you. It may take them a while, but at least you will be alive.

Tamping down your fixation on a quick escape or rescue goes hand in hand with pausing to let adrenaline subside. Many of the cases we have used to illustrate the importance of these two mindsets focused on solitary survivors. But if you are in a group setting, how can you have a calming effect on others, or take on a leadership role with the "steady strain" philosophy? You do it by example. The next stories illustrate how one's demeanor is contagious.

In an earlier chapter you met JP, Ben, and Rudy, who had to abandon their sinking sailboat in a storm and board a damaged life raft. We saw the decisions made that helped them stay alive as long as possible, but only a Coast Guard helicopter crew could ultimately save them. That team on the helicopter had to fly 250 miles out to sea in hurricane-force winds and extract three men from rampaging waves averaging sixty feet, with some as high as eighty feet. A rescue doesn't get more difficult than that.

Nevada Smith was the aircraft's commander, Aaron Nelson the copilot, Drew Dazzo the rescue swimmer, and Scott Higgins the hoist operator. When they arrived on scene [a C-130 plane had previously located the raft, a miracle in itself], Nevada could hardly believe what he was seeing. The life raft looked miniscule, the size of a dime, in the maw of a seventy-foot wave. He watched as the top part of the wave lifted the raft so high it looked like it was on a mountaintop, and then it teetered there for a second before plunging down the wave's back side into the valley below.

The other crew members were just as awestruck...and concerned. Scott's first thought was that the raft was flying along at six knots and how difficult that would make it to lower and extract Drew, the rescue swimmer. For his part, Drew focused on the waves, not so much their size, but how steep they were and how they broke like an avalanche. *If I get buried by one of those, it's going to push me down like a pile driver.*

Aaron was flying the chopper, and he lowered it to 120 feet from the wave troughs. He positioned the helicopter just behind the raft so the tiny vessel didn't take the full brunt of the rotor wash, which caused the water below the aircraft to look like a blizzard. Blasts of wind slammed the helo, making it near impossible to hold position, and the life raft was often out of view before one of the airmen spotted it again.

While interviewing the four-man helicopter crew, what impressed me most, besides their teamwork, was how each of them had a calming effect on the other. When one person's adrenaline was spiking, another would tamp it down, almost in a casual manner. No shouting, no berating, no barking orders.

As Drew was thinking about how to descend to the raft, he thought he could save time by jumping into the water without being lowered by the cable. The wave tops came near the hovering helicopter, and if he timed his jump for when a wave was closest, Drew thought a simple plunge was doable. Through his headset he said to Nevada, "Can we do a free-fall deployment?"

Nevada paused for a minute, knowing the free fall would be a bit riskier than being lowered by the cable.

"Do you really think that's the safest way to enter the water?" he asked Drew. Notice Nevada did not say no right off the bat, but instead wanted to let Drew come to the same conclusion. He also knew that Drew's adrenaline was sky-high—it had to be to voluntarily enter such a maelstrom.

This short exchange gave Drew the time he needed to override the adrenaline surge that was shouting HURRY! He had to act quickly and decisively, but not in a rush.

Drew replied to Nevada: "You're right."

The rescue would take whatever time was needed. That might be until they get all three men out of the water, or if low fuel forced them to leave before the mission was complete, they might have to exit with only one or two survivors. It seemed cruel, but it would be crueler to have both rescuers and survivors perish.

The four-man crew did their best, despite the chaos around them, to take the long view. They didn't need to just get the three men on the raft back to land, they had four others as well—themselves. And so they used their training and a certain tone in their voices to stay steady—or, as John McCain said, "steady strain." While McCain emphasized that you don't want your emotions on a roller coaster, the men in the raft and those in helo all *felt* like they were on one, with the enormous waves and bruising wind gusts. But that didn't mean their emotions had to follow.

As Scott prepared to lower Drew, Aaron, flying the aircraft, watched the radar altimeter reading go from one hundred feet to twenty. His eyes widened because he knew that meant an eighty-foot wave had just passed beneath the aircraft. Aaron's number one concern was having a large wave sneak up on him and clip the helo.

When I interviewed Aaron, he shared how at that moment he said to himself, *Stay relaxed, we have time. If it takes more than one attempt to get the first man, that's okay.* He wasn't going to allow the adrenaline to rush him and force a mistake.

Nevada had seen the same huge wave, and told Aaron he would start calling out the big waves. And later when he did see one monstrous wall of water approaching, he was careful not to shout it out, but instead said three words in the calmest voice possible: "Big wave coming." He knew Aaron was under enough stress just trying to fly the aircraft, and there was no need to add to it.

Drew used a similar approach when he finally reached the men in the raft. He spat the snorkel out of his mouth, looked at the sailors, and said, "How y'all doing today?"

Rudy was in shock that anyone could swim in seas so huge and shouted, "You guys are fucking amazing!"

Drew said thank you, and then asked if anyone was injured. Rescue swimmers always take the person who is hurt or cannot swim first, knowing they may require the most energy from the rescue swimmer, so he should do it while fresh. And so Drew gently slid JP from the raft and said, "We're going for a basket ride."

Language matters. Demeanor matters. Even facial expression. Though the Coast Guard men knew time was of the essence because of fuel considerations, they tried not to appear rushed.

With the waves so chaotic, Drew had trouble getting JP in the basket, and after one near-miss the basket blew far away. All Drew could do was wait for Aaron, Nevada, and Scott to do their parts to reposition the aircraft and the basket.

Scott thought, *This is taking too long. Wonder what the fuel situation is…* But he stopped himself. *That's the pilot's concern. Just do your job.*

All three sailors were eventually saved, but not before some tense moments trying to get Drew, the last one in the water, back in the aircraft.

When they were back on land, the sickening after-effect of so much adrenaline coursing through their bodies was most pronounced. Aaron told me that, upon arriving home, he walked into the living room and lay down on the floor. His wife massaged his temples, and he began telling her what had happened, choking up, surprised at his reaction. Like the others, he stayed calm through the ordeal, and only after it was all over did he allow "steady strain" to end and emotion to take over.

Over the years, I've interviewed many Coast Guard pilots who have had to fly in horrendous weather. Prior to getting involved with these pilots, I envisioned them as the *Top Gun/Rambo* types who cut corners and flew by the seat of their pants to make incredible rescues. Nothing could be further from the truth. They are assessing risk throughout their mission, ready to abort if that's what the situation dictates. Although their goal is to make the rescue, the pilots have an even more important priority and responsibility: to keep their crew from harm. What good does it do to perform an incredible rescue only to have the helicopter go down on the return flight? They might push the envelope to save lives, but every decision they make takes the long view, and the safety of the crew is paramount. Pilots don't have the luxury to just focus on the rescue part of the mission, but instead have to think about getting back to land safely when conditions are changing by the minute.

One pilot who impressed me during the rescue of the crew of the tall ship *Bounty* was Steve Cerveny. In an interesting twist of fate, he also knew what it was like to be a survivor. Steve has both saved lives and had his own life saved. His story is one of resilience and taking the long view.

Steve's accident occurred in 2010 when he was the copilot in a Coast Guard Jayhawk helicopter. He and his crew were traveling over a remote, mountainous region of Utah after providing security in a joint US-Canadian operation for the Winter Olympics in Vancouver, British Columbia.

Light snow had been falling during the prior half-hour over Utah, and some was sticking to the aircraft, forcing the pilots to activate the engine anti-icing mechanism. A lead helicopter was flying just ahead of Steve's, and it had disappeared into a cloud bank. Somewhere in front of them was a ridgeline Steve knew they must fly over.

The aircraft commander was flying the 20,000-pound helicopter from the left seat, and Steve was in the right. As the commander tried to gain altitude to crest the 10,000-foot ridgeline, the Jayhawk was not responding. Steve called for more airspeed, realizing the anti-icing mechanism was robbing them of power. The commander tried to increase altitude, but when the helicopter did not respond, he immediately turned away from the mountain tops. Banking hard to the right, both men were horrified to see treetops emerge from the blizzard just a few feet in front of them. The rotors clipped the trees and in a split second the giant steel bird lurched to a stop and plummeted sideways, crashing through splintering pines and into the snow.

When the helicopter finally came to rest, Steve felt a searing pain shooting through his leg. He looked for the commander who should have been in the seat to his left. Instead he saw only snow.

Steve released his safety harness and tried to stand. That's when he noticed the lower part of his leg was turned inward at a forty-five-degree angle and blood was seeping through his pants.

The commander's head popped out of the snow, but he too was injured, both men trapped in the steaming, hissing aircraft that could ignite at any moment. In the rear of the helicopter, basic air crewmember Gina Panuzzi was critically hurt, with severe internal injuries. Luckily, rescue swimmer Darren Hicks and flight mechanic Edward Sychra were relatively unscathed and started pulling the injured from the wreckage, which was scattered over hundreds of feet, including up in the trees.

The accident had happened so quickly that no emergency call could be made, and the lead helicopter pilots that had been in front of Steve's aircraft didn't know they had gone down. Now, the five survivors were in a race against time; their injuries and hypothermia would sap their strength and soon snuff out their lives.

Flight mechanic Edward Sychra used his cell phone to send a text message to the flight mechanic of the lead helicopter. The text was received and the flight mechanic in the lead copter texted back that they were alerting authorities and were going to land as close to the crash site as possible. Meanwhile, Steve's open compound fracture was causing excruciating pain, and the rescue swimmer did his best to use a tree branch as a splint. Steve thought, *Well, I'm responsible for getting us into this jam, and maybe now God is going to help us get out of it.* Despite the pain he felt, a calmness come over him, and his thoughts turned to the more seriously injured Gina Panuzzi. He knew she needed medical attention immediately.

A short time later, the lead helicopter returned, but the giant H-60 was incapable of hovering at that altitude. Pilot Steven Bonn flew to a lower altitude and lightened the aircraft by dumping fuel, then he returned to the crash site and in an amazing display of skill, somehow guided the helicopter down into a confined opening in the woods, just a couple hundred yards below the crash site. A med-flight helicopter also landed nearby, and the injured were whisked off to Salt Lake City. Snowmobilers also arrived on scene, and they took Sychra and rescue swimmer Hicks down off the mountain.

When Steve was identified as one of the injured, authorities called his mother. The pilot's mother had the same feeling Steve had on the mountain; that her son would pull through. The date of the accident—March 3—had significance for her. This was the day her infant daughter had died years earlier. *God's not going to take two away,* she told herself. *Steve is being watched over and will be fine.*

Steve did pull through, but he wasn't fine. He had surgery on his leg, but his orthopedic doctor warned him he could still lose the limb. After a month on his back in the hospital, a second surgery was performed that included bone grafts and the bitter news that he might not be able to ever put weight on his leg, and that his flying days were likely over. *I'm in God's hands now,* reasoned Steve, *I'm at peace with what happens.* He decided not to set a deadline for his goal of walking again. *It's going to happen, I just don't know when. I'll do my part for as long as it takes.*

While recuperating, Steve went over the rescue events and counted several things that had to go just as they did for him and the others not to have died. First, they landed in an incredible nine feet of snow, softening the impact and reducing the risk of fire. Second, in hundreds of miles of woods, they crashed just 200 yards from a clearing. And third, pilot Bonn managed to maneuver his helicopter into the opening despite the difficulty of hovering in such an altitude. Steve thought of several other factors, such as had the accident happened at night, they would not have been found in time. *I think God had a plan,* he thought, *and now I'm going to follow that plan and give it my best.* He thought of how pilots like himself, who fly into dangerous situations and need confidence, but in the big scheme of things there are factors beyond control, and faith can get you through the toughest of times.

For the next several months Steve directed his energy into physical therapy, and with each step he began to realize he might someday fly again. Approximately a year and a half after the accident, in October of 2011, Steve was behind the controls of a Jayhawk, and throttled the helicopter off the tarmac and into the sky.

The story of Steve Cerveny's comeback from the trauma and injuries of the crash is inspiring. But what happened next—one year after his first post-accident flight—is truly amazing. In the early morning hours of October 29, 2012, Steve was called on to fly into the teeth of Superstorm Sandy. The tall ship HMS *Bounty*, a replica of the ship from *Mutiny on the Bounty*, was sinking, and the sailors had abandoned the vessel and were fighting for survival in the storm-tossed seas.

Steve's crew consisted of copilot Jane Pena, flight mechanic Michael Lufkin, and rescue swimmer Randy Haba. A C-130 search plane was already on the scene, and the helicopter crew knew the situation with the *Bounty's* crew was critical. As Steve's aircraft approached the coordinates of the sinking *Bounty*, he lowered the helicopter to a hundred feet above the angry ocean. The first thing he noticed was blinking strobe lights scattered about.

Steve slowly decreased their altitude, and with night-vision goggles, he and his crew investigated the lights flashing below them. The first two or three were attached to survival suits, but the suits were empty. [The lights were water-activated strobe lights.] The C-130 pilots directed the helo to another strobe light about a half mile away. This time the arm of the survival suit slowly rose from the water, and the helo crew could see a hand.

Flight mechanic Michael Lufkin lowered swimmer Randy Haba on the cable into the thirty-foot seas. The plan was for Haba to stay attached to the cable and put the survivor in a sling, and the two would be lifted back to the helicopter together. The waves, however, were not going to allow such an easy rescue.

Haba swam toward the drifting survivor and was almost within reach when a breaking sea buried him and he was jerked backward by the cable. Now Lufkin would have to direct Steve to maneuver the helicopter into a better position so Haba would be closer to the survivor—no easy feat in a hurricane.

Again Haba swam for the survivor, and again the combination of a breaking wave and the cable carried Haba backward. Steve knew they had to get this survivor up fast—he had been pounded by seas for over an hour since abandoning the *Bounty*, and no one knew how much longer he could keep his head above the boiling seas. Every year of Steve's training and flight experience would have to be marshaled to get the helicopter in the perfect position, and then hold it in a stationary hover while being buffeted by severe wind gusts.

On the third attempt, the swimmer reached the survivor and put him in the sling, and they were safely lifted into the belly of the helicopter. There was no time for celebration; the C-130 pilot had just informed Steve over the radio that they had located a life raft. Steve banked the big iron bird, and off they went toward what they hoped would be survivors in the raft.

On the way, a hint of gray dawn allowed for a quick glimpse of an eerie scene that seemed to be out of a century-old past. The *Bounty*, with decks awash, was half submerged in the ocean, its masts sticking almost straight up. A blinking strobe light was in the rigging, and Steve lowered the helo, excitement building in hopes of having located another survivor. But as they descended down to fifty feet above the mast, the crew realized once again it was an empty survival suit whose water-activated light was flashing. Steve held the helo in place, and the crew looked for signs of life in the wreckage surrounding the ship, but found none. For a split second, Steve flashed back to the wreckage of his helo on the mountain. He now knew why he was spared; he and his crew had to save more lives. He banked the helicopter in the direction of the life raft.

When they were in a hover above the raft, Randy Haba went down on the hook, this time detaching from it when he reached the water. He knifed through the ocean to the raft, and upon reaching the door was relieved to see heads poking out, eyes wide as saucers.

Steve and his crew started extracting survivors from the raft, but they were low on fuel long before they could pluck all the survivors from the churning ocean. Over the headset, Steve, in a calm voice, said "We're at Bingo. After we get the swimmer up, we're going home."

When Randy was hauled back in the helo, he was told "RTB" (return to base). He responded, "We still got three people down there!"

Steve had to take the long view. It didn't matter how many people were still in the stormy seas. If they ran out of fuel, everyone in the helo would perish. Then Steve heard the most welcome voice on the radio—it was the pilot of another Coast Guard helicopter arriving at the scene. The voice was very familiar to Steve. Incredibly, the pilot of this second aircraft was Steven Bonn, the same pilot who had helped extract the injured crew from the crash on the mountain two and half years earlier.

Of the sixteen sailors on the Bounty, fourteen had survived the capsizing. The crews of commanders Steve Cerveny and Steven Bonn managed to rescue all fourteen in conditions far worse than what they had experienced in the mountains of Utah.

On the flight back to Coast Guard Air Station Elizabeth City, Steve relinquished the controls of the aircraft to copilot Jane Pena. Steve had a moment to think about the rescue. *This type of rescue just doesn't happen very often in the Coast Guard. Everything had to go just right for us to save so many in such conditions.*

It was very similar to the incredibly good fortune Steve's crashed crew on the Utah mountains had, except this time it was Steve doing the rescuing.

## SURVIVOR LESSONS FOR YOUR LIFE:

- Keep the hope that good things are coming, but don't set an artificial deadline. Instead, have the mindset that you will do your best for however long it (change, luck, salvation, success) takes.

- John McCain stressed the importance of staying even-keeled (he called it "steady strain"), rather than getting hopes up for a quick fix which can send you on a roller coaster ride that usually ends badly. He also pointed out that, during adversity, isolation is the enemy, so reach out to others—force yourself if you have to, but don't go it alone.

- Don't let the pressure of the situation rush your actions. Your priority is to get it right rather than going for expediency. By taking the long view of the situation, your decisions will be more sound.

## CHAPTER 13

# FINAL THOUGHTS

My thirty-year quest of interviewing and researching extreme survivors has taught me that they do share some common traits, which have nothing to do with their physical power or education. Instead, it is how they first perceive the situation and then mentally react to the stress it produces. If I had to use one word to describe their response to a dire predicament, that word would be *composure*. They may be rattled and afraid, but the fear does not stop their minds from gathering information and then assessing various options to improve their circumstances. Where I might panic and my stress force me into hasty actions, the extreme survivors who accomplish the near-miraculous seem as if they can slow time down while considering what they need to do next.

Many of the extreme survivors we have analyzed in the preceding chapters would be solid leaders—not so much by what they say, but by the manner in which they act. If there are other people caught in the same emergency, the composure exhibited by an extreme survivor has a calming effect on them. Keeping your cool in the midst of chaos is perhaps the best leadership skill there is.

Every single survivor (and extreme rescuer) who I interviewed over the years had a humbleness about them, and most were soft-spoken, with a wry sense of humor. This is why an article written by Sam Walker of the *Wall Street Journal* caught my eye. The article was titled "In a Life-or-Death Crisis, Humility is Everything," And it focused on an incident that occurred many years ago aboard a United Airlines flight. Captain Alfred Haynes was piloting the aircraft when the tail engine exploded, causing shrapnel to sever all the plane's hydraulics, making the flaps and rudders inoperable. Haynes calmly asked the copilot to look up the procedure for steering the plane under these circumstances. "There is none," he replied.

Haynes considered his limited options. He still had two functioning wing engines, and he and his three-man crew were able to work the throttle on those and allow the plane to descend toward a nearby airport in Sioux City, Iowa. But their speed—250 miles per hour—was double the normal landing velocity for a DC-10, and the aircraft was without working brakes. It would seem the plane, and everyone in it, didn't have a chance.

When the plane crash-landed and broke into four pieces, 184 of the 296 people on board survived, including Captain Haynes. Later, after recovering from his injuries, he answered questions from the media. One of his comments could have been uttered by any one of the extreme survivors I've interviewed, because it showed both humility and gratitude for the other members of the flight team who assisted him during this nightmare flight. "There is no hero," said Haynes, "there is just a group of four people who did their job."

Captain Haynes also showed another trait the survivors I worked with possessed during the darkest times: humor. When Haynes was keeping his cool while the jet was aloft and drifting from side to side, he was told he was cleared to land on any runway at Sioux City. His response? He chuckled and replied, "You want to be particular and make it a runway, huh?"

Humility, composure, and humor (even gallows humor) mixed with quiet confidence is a winning formula for overcoming adversity and leading others in times of crisis. This combination can keep one focused to give them a fighting chance at a successful outcome. I call this the "survivor vibe." But this overall feeling requires specific techniques for the uniqueness of each individual situation. And that's what we will review next.

Let's take a look at how extreme survivors handle an emergency from the very beginning of the ordeal to the end. This chronological order of how their brain deals with what is happening to them—and around them—can be useful for all of us during a period of adversity. Our difficulties may not have the life-or-death immediacy that these survivors were faced with, but their actions provide a road map for when the rest of us are under duress and feel overwhelmed.

When a dangerous event is unfolding, some will be in denial and proceed as if nothing has changed. Maybe we hesitate because we are in a group situation and don't want to be the one to suggest a change in plans or spoil the fun. Or maybe there is someone in the group with more expertise, and so we defer to them even when every neuron in our body is telling us we are facing a threat and in jeopardy. Yet another reason for ignoring warning signs is that they are often vague—a gut feeling can be hard to explain to others, or even rationalize to ourselves.

Instead of sweeping our concerns under the rug, this is where we need to stop and confront the situation head-on. The first step is to try and identify what is bothering you: Is it the actions of another person? Is it a change in external conditions? Or is it the feeling that you are committing yourself to a perilous path, where your options to abort or make adjustments are becoming fewer and fewer? Whatever the reason, this is the time to talk about what you're feeling with the group (or with yourself if you are alone). Tell yourself you will not be *blinded by the goal* to such an extent that you commit to a certain path to achieve it. Remind yourself that the goal will be there for another day. Yes, the goal is of importance to you, but how you reach it should be fluid and subject to change based on the latest information. Think of your brain as a completely objective computer: it's pulling in all the latest data, analyzing it, and finally formulating a new course of action if warranted. This objective assessment might protect you from harm, or at the very least mitigate the damage coming your way.

But suppose the event is like a trap that envelopes you with little warning, leaving you with only one option: deal with it as best you can. This is what happened to Ernie Hazard on that cold November day in the North Atlantic when the 90- to 100-foot wave hit the *Fair Wind* and the boat capsized. I use Ernie as an example because he had to make several critical decisions over the course of his ordeal to survive. And he had to get every decision right. It was not like taking a test, where you can score 95 out of 100 and still get an A. He had to get 100 percent. Ernie is also a good case study because, like the pilot Alfred Haynes of the DC-10, he exhibited the same extreme survivor traits of humility and composure. Ernie's determination to not give up, but instead [even when all seemed lost] stay with the mindset of "I'm going to go down fighting," is nothing short of remarkable.

Thinking back on Ernie's ordeal, it occurred to me that he used almost every technique we have discussed in this book to survive. In a sense, I look at Ernie as the ultimate extreme survivor. [Ernie would disagree, I'm sure, because of his humble nature, and he would attribute his ultimate outcome to many instances of luck. And yes, there were a couple of lucky breaks, but it's what he did with that luck—and what he did with the bad cards dealt his way— that makes him exceptional.]

When I first learned about Ernie tumbling in the life raft, I thought there was nothing more Ernie could do to affect his chances of survival other than try to stay inside the raft. But while he couldn't control external events, he could choose his response to the bleak situation. He had the option of simply giving up and ending the pain he was in, from the effects of hypothermia and the mental terror of being lost 200 miles out at sea with little hope of survival. Or he could endure for as long as it took until help arrived. He chose the latter and put his resourcefulness to work—for example, when the raft flipped upside down, he swam out and crawled into the ballast bag. Throughout his ordeal, he gave himself pep talks, repeating phrases like, "Good job, Ernie. Just get through the next hour."

Throughout his two and half days in the life raft, he kept his mind as busy as he could, experimenting with positions that would better keep him inside the raft when a big wave hit, or repeatedly reading the directions on the flare gun to make sure he knew how to shoot it if help came. He would string the power of these little steps like these along to keep doing whatever was in his power to improve his circumstances. And when negative thoughts entered his mind that the odds of rescue were infinitesimal, he'd push them away and tell himself he needed to live so that the families of his crewmates would know what happened. Thinking of others was yet one more reason to endure. *I'm going to pull this off,* he told himself on his second frigid night in the raft. *I didn't spend all this time fighting just to give up now.*

While Ernie was too hypothermic and exhausted to use humor in his ordeal, it was there when he was rescued by a Coast Guard cutter. The waves had decreased considerably since the sinking of the *Fair Wind*, but some chairs in the galley still slid around when a big wave hit the vessel. The young Coastie who was escorting Ernie to the sick bay said, "If you think this is bad, you should have been here yesterday." Ernie deadpanned back, "I would have liked that very much."

Ernie has had many years to look back on his terrible ordeal in the life raft. He says his survival experience did not greatly change him. However, he did point out a more subtle adjustment to the way he views challenges, saying, "These are free years I'm living. And so I don't let the little stuff get to me. And when bigger problems come along, I figure somehow I'll solve them. Although I don't always make the best of these extra years, I am surely thankful for each and every day."

During my research, I tried to see if the very best survivors had a common trait or common experience in their lives before their ordeal. One feature jumped out at me: nearly all had spent time alone during their younger years and were not afraid to try a difficult venture on their own. For example, Ernie rode a bicycle from Canada to Mexico (alone); JP learned sailing from fisherman he met at his local pier, then found an abandoned boat, fixed it up, and sailed alone; and Loch went on a solo hitch-hiking trip for many days, from Long Island up through Canada. Loch, who was sixteen years old, slept in the woods by the side of the road. When a car stopped to pick him up, the driver would ask, "Where are you going?" and Loch would ask, "Well, where are you headed?" And when Loch got the answer, he often said, "I think I'll go there."

My guess is that solitary journeys like these in the teenage years built confidence. They reinforced the notion that these individuals could solve problems on their own, and that they were comfortable being alone. So when disaster struck later in life, and they found themselves alone with no prospect of help arriving quickly, they could draw on that inner self-reliance and keep panic at bay. Sure, they had fear like we all do, but they were able to act despite it. This concept was put another way by Medal of Honor recipient Woodrow Wilson Keeble, a Native American who fought courageously during both WWII and the Korean War. He said, "I did not let my fear make a coward out of me."

In their teenage years, most of the extreme survivors were constantly curious, always seeking to understand how things work, always interested in a new experience. In many instances they exhibited traits of a true maverick, marching to their own drummer, chafing at rules that made little sense or group pressure to conform. (Louis Zamperini of *Unbroken* fame is a good example.) Many were technically competent and able to fix defective man-made objects. (Anyone who knows me also knows I'd make a poor survivor, as my technical skills are nil and my curiosity doesn't prompt me to understand the inner workings of an item.] The best extreme survivors approach problems analytically and rationally.

Extreme survivors are most definitely not rigid people, but instead are adaptable and creative, with inquiring minds that allow them to easily leave comfort zones to explore new places and acquire new friends. They do not need a road map to chart their own course, nor is achieving "security" high on their priority list. While some of us flourish in a work environment where a manager tells us when, how, and why to do things, the maverick/extreme survivor succeeds because they have the personal discipline to prioritize what needs to be done next.

After a brief conversation with Dodge Morgan, the first American to sail solo around the globe with no stops, I read his book, *Voyage of America's Promise*. At the back was a section titled, "A Psychological Portrait of a Solo Circumnavigator." Before his epic journey, two PhDs conducted a battery of tests on him over eight days. The outcomes of the tests were quite similar to my observations about extreme survivors. The doctors said the portrait that emerged "could aptly be titled *Thick-Skinned Individualist*." I thought it was the perfect label for character traits I'd zeroed in on with the survivors I knew best.

Another section of the psychological summary also highlighted a common trait amongst these problem-solving survivors. It read, "Morgan has spent his life pursuing independence: he cherishes self-assertion and self-sufficiency. Morgan also relishes playing the role of a nonconformist who does not readily accept the conventions, rules, and standards of others. Nor does he rely heavily on others for emotional support."

What is clear to me is that extreme survivors make the most of their limited resources and then patiently let their I-can-solve-most-problems attitude go to work on improving their odds.

But what about the rest of us, who may not have any of these traits, or have just one or two? Luckily, most of us will not find ourselves in the immediate life-or-death situations the people in this book experienced, but we will encounter adversity, whether it be a job loss, divorce, illness, or a myriad of other gut punches. During these times of stress, we can think back on the mindsets detailed in this book and chose from the following list to emerge from the ordeal stronger, and with a brighter future. Here are some of the phrases and techniques I've used in my own life when I was knocked down or when one of my goals seemed almost unattainable:

## AS LONG AS IT TAKES

Don't expect miracles, or feeling like your old self to return, in a short period of time. Instead, take the approach of "As Long As It Takes," knowing your efforts are incrementally leading you to the other side. Think of yourself as a stonemason trying to break a rock a certain way. You don't just slam it with a maul, but instead chip away at it. You may not see the result of each little blow, but suddenly one of them splits the stone. Was it the last one that did it, or was it the accumulation of all your chips? It's the accumulation, but you just don't know exactly when results will appear.

## THINKING OF OTHERS

You may not feel like acting a certain way, but thinking of others who are or were important in your life can bring out the best in you. If I encounter a really big bump in my journey, I think of my father and mother, and how they handled adversity with grace. Or I think of my kids and how I want to set a good example showing I can take a punch, keep my head down, and do the next right thing.

## HELP FROM WITHIN & BEYOND

Extreme survivors do not share a common spiritual belief system. I find that encouraging, because it means that, no matter your religion or beliefs, you can find what works best for you. Some said they prayed, others said they knew they were on their own. My technique is to use a combination of the two: I'll ask God/A Higher Power/The Universe/The Great Creator to give me strength [not to solve the problem], and I'll do my best to endure and eventually triumph.

## THE POWER OF LITTLE STEPS

The power of little steps is the way to go. Even the smallest bit of action can get the ball rolling toward fulfillment. Noteworthy accomplishments are rarely gained without behind-the-scenes preparation that might feel insignificant at the time but, taken together with other little steps, sends you toward your goal.

When I feel overwhelmed by a project, I break it down into smaller pieces. Many people who start writing a book give up quickly when they think how far away the finished product is. My solution has always been to focus solely on the chapter I'm writing. Each chapter has its own file of notes and ideas, and those become my world. When I'm done with a chapter, I take a break [I really should celebrate], and it's not until all the chapters are finished that I review them and start a careful rewrite so they flow. Extreme survivors taught me that you can get overwhelmed when thinking about how much work you have in front of you, and that the best approach is to focus on just the next hour or two.

## PEP TALKS & THE POSSIBILITY OF LUCK

Don't wait for others to give you a pat on the back—it may never come. When faced with a difficult period in your life, be like the extreme survivors who celebrated even the smallest of achievements. And be on the lookout for a piece of good luck, and make the most of it.

## OPTIONS

Most of the extreme survivors in this book experienced their ordeal alone. In everyday life, you are almost never alone—lean on friends, family, or a therapist to help you see the many options in front of you. Examine the problem from all perspectives; that may ignite a new course of action, an inner resourcefulness that might surprise you.

## PAUSE IF TIME ALLOWS

Not all situations allow for a long pause, but take full advantage of extra time if you don't need to respond right away. That lets the emotion and adrenaline dissipate, and you view the situation in a more measured way.

## MINIMIZE THE TIME SPENT THINKING OF MISTAKES

Suspend the past and future and instead do "the next right thing." One survivor trait that surfaces time and time again is that true survivors do not waste time thinking about how they got into such a position or who to blame. Nor do they waste time pondering the distant future, which might lead to "what's the use" syndrome. Instead, they look at what they need to do now, which moves them one step closer to their goal.

## A PHRASE TO LIVE BY

Abolish the detrimental thinking that says "I'll be happy when..." That way of thinking is a fool's errand because you give up the sure thing [today] for an uncertainty [tomorrow].

Replace that outlook with one of gratitude. I use the phrase "Thank you for putting me on the path to _____ [fill in the blank]." With this mindset, you are giving thanks for the journey while being hopeful about the result. Enjoy the challenge of the process, the personal growth that comes with it, and not just the outcome.

Working with extreme survivors has been beneficial for me in so many ways, and now it can be for you as well.

# A THANK YOU

A big thank you to the team who helped make this a better book: Nicole Resciniti, Julie Gwinn, Brenda Knight, Veronica Diaz, Geena El-Haj, and Chris H.

And of course I am grateful to all the survivors: not just the survivors I cite in the sources, but many others who I've interviewed and were gracious with their time.

Extreme survivors who share their experience give the rest of us valuable life lessons. Even if we never use a single technique in this book, when we read about their ordeals, it should ignite in us the quest to enjoy each and every day. We know that life can change in an instant, and if it does, these extreme survivors show us how to manage the situation as best we can and make it to the other side. They all shared their stories, opened their hearts, and gave us survival lessons we can all use.

# APPENDIX

For those readers who are interested in the way JFK came to his decision during the Cuban Missile Crisis—and the way he conducted his meetings—I've outlined fourteen steps he took that would be helpful in any major decision.

## ONE: "HOW MUCH TIME DO WE HAVE?"

Upon first learning that the Soviets were erecting nuclear missile launch sites, the President wanted to know when the missiles would be operational. This would establish the time frame of how long he had to make a decision and implement that decision.

## TWO: ESTABLISH WHO WILL COMPRISE THE CORE TEAM OF ADVISORS.

Kennedy immediately selected his team of advisors on the Executive Committee, ExComm. He chose a diverse group, not all "yes men."

## THREE: WHY DID THIS HAPPEN? / PUT YOURSELF IN YOUR ADVERSARY'S POSITION.

Kennedy put himself in adversary's position to understand motives. He recognized that Khrushchev could even the playing field with missiles close to the US, as the US had in Turkey. Understanding your adversary helps guide you to a win-win solution.

## FOUR: ESTABLISH THE GOAL QUICKLY, BUT NOT THE STEPS TO GET THERE.

Kennedy's goal was simple: the missiles must go. But the plan— the way to achieve this goal—was left open. The President had established a time frame (two weeks) so he would not be rushed.

## FIVE: SEEK CLARITY OF OPTIONS SO ALL GROUP MEMBERS HAVE THE SAME UNDERSTANDING.

As soon as Kennedy realized that he had failed to clearly label the options, he stopped everyone at his initial meeting to make sure they got on the same page.

## SIX: KENNEDY ASKED EACH MEMBER OF THE GROUP TO CONSIDER WHAT THEY THOUGHT THE CONSEQUENCES WOULD BE ON EACH POTENTIAL COURSE OF ACTION.

All decisions have consequences, and it's important to try to anticipate them.

## SEVEN: PLAY DEVIL'S ADVOCATE—PUSH MEMBERS TO VIEW THE SITUATION FROM EVERY POSSIBLE ANGLE.

The President said, "Say the situation was reversed..." and phrases like that to get his team to look at the problem from all angles.

## EIGHT: BE WARY OF EACH TEAM MEMBER'S MOTIVES.

In other words: could leaders of the military be pushing a certain course of action partly because of career considerations?

## NINE: GIVE ALL MEMBERS A CHANCE TO COMMENT BEFORE MAKING A DECISION.

Don't let one or two senior people dominate the meeting, or soon everyone will be just following them, and a great option might be missed.

## TEN: ALLOW MAVERICKS TO BE MAVERICKS.

Kennedy wanted to hear all ideas, even from Curtis LeMay, who was borderline insubordinate during the Cuban Missile Crisis meetings.

## ELEVEN: USE HUMOR TO DEFUSE TENSION.

At one point in the meetings, LeMay tried to ratchet up the pressure on the President to take bold action.

> **LeMay:** I think that a blockade, and political talk, would be considered by a lot of our friends and neutrals as being a pretty weak response to this. And I'm sure a lot of our own citizens would feel that way too. You're in a pretty bad fix, Mr. President.
>
> **President Kennedy:** Re-say it?
>
> **LeMay:** You're in a pretty bad fix.
>
> **Kennedy:** You're in it with me.

## TWELVE: WORRY ABOUT UNINTENDED CONSEQUENCES AND MISUNDERSTANDINGS.

JFK was inspired by a book he had just read, *The Guns of August*, by Barbara Tuchman, which chronicled how World War I started. This Pulitzer Prize-winning book illuminated how nations can tumble into war, not so much by strategy as by reactions to events. The President drew the parallel that if he launched surprise air strikes, the Soviets would have no option but to respond, and soon the dominoes of reactions would start falling on the way to all-out nuclear war, which neither side wanted. The President and his brother Bobby even talked about the book during the crisis, with the President emphasizing how simple miscalculations led to consequences few had foreseen. Bobby later recalled that his brother pointed out how "stupidity, individual idiosyncrasies, misunderstandings, and personal complexes of inferiority and grandeur" all had led to responses and counter-responses that escalated. Writing in his book *Thirteen Days*, Bobby explained that the President did not want to "challenge the other side needlessly, or precipitously push our adversaries into a course of action that was not intended or anticipated."

## THIRTEEN: IF POSSIBLE, CHOOSE THE COURSE OF ACTION THAT CAN BE DONE IN STEPS AND ALLOWS THE MOST FLEXIBILITY.

While the Joint Chiefs preferred an immediate air strike on every military installation in Cuba, Kennedy decided that move should only be implemented if all else failed, because it would likely lead to war. His first decision was to start with the blockade and see if that got the desired results, and follow that up with secret negotiations.

## FOURTEEN: DON'T FEAR REVERSING YOUR COURSE.

Kennedy had said that if a plane was shot down, he would order an immediate air strike against the SAM site that fired. But when Major Rudy Anderson's U-2 was shot down, the President did not act. Instead, he made a last offer to the Soviets for a deal.

# ABOUT THE AUTHOR

**Michael J. Tougias** [pronounced *Toh-Gis*, hard G] is a lecturer and *New York Times* bestselling author and coauthor of thirty-one books for adults and eight for young adults and children.

*Fatal Forecast: An Incredible True Tale of Disaster and Survival at Sea* was praised by the *Los Angeles Times* as "a breathtaking book—Tougias spins a marvelous and terrifying story." *The Finest Hours,* which Tougias coauthored, tells the true story of the Coast Guard's most daring rescue. A finalist for the Massachusetts Book Award, the book was made into a movie by Disney. *Ten Hours Until Dawn: The True Story of Heroism and Tragedy Aboard the Can Do in the Blizzard of 78* was selected by the American Library Association as one of the "Top Books of the Year" and described as a "white-knuckle read, the best book of its kind." His latest books are *A Storm Too Soon, Above & Beyond,* and a prequel to *There's a Porcupine in My Outhouse* titled *The Waters Between Us: A Boy, A Father, Outdoor Misadventures, and the Healing Power of Nature.*

Several of Tougias's books were adapted for middle readers [ages eight to thirteen] and for chapter books with MacMillan Publishers. His True Rescue series includes *Into the Blizzard, Attacked At Sea, A Storm Too Soon, The Finest Hours,* and *Rescue of the Bounty*

Michael Tougias has been featured on ABC's *20/20,* the Weather Channel, National Public Radio, and The Travel Channel, among other appearances. He offers slide lectures for each of his books and speaks at libraries, lecture series, schools, and colleges across the country. He also speaks to business groups and associations on leadership and decision-making, including such programs as Leadership Lessons from the Finest Hours; Survival Lessons: Decision Making Under Pressure; and Fourteen Steps to Strategic Decision Making: JFK and the Cuban Missile Crisis. He lives in

Florida and Massachusetts. For more information, to view videos of some of the rescues Tougias writes about, or to contact the author, visit www.michaeltougias.com. On Facebook, you can find him at Author Michael J. Tougias.

### Tougias's most popular books include:

- *No Will Set You Free: You're One Bad Habit Away from Happiness*

- *Rescue of the Bounty: A True Story of Disaster and Survival in Superstorm Sandy*, Simon & Schuster, coauthor Douglas Campbell

- *A Storm Too Soon: A True Story of Disaster, Survival, and an Incredible Rescue*, Simon & Schuster

- *Overboard! A True Blue-Water Odyssey of Disaster and Survival*, Simon & Schuster

- *Fatal Forecast: An Incredible True Story of Disaster and Survival at Sea*, Simon & Schuster

- *Ten Hours Until Dawn: The True Story of Heroism and Tragedy Aboard the Can Do*, St. Martin's Press, American Library Association Best Book of the Year Selection

- *The Finest Hours: The True Story of the US Coast Guard's Most Daring Sea Rescue*, Simon & Schuster, coauthor Casey Sherman, finalist for the Massachusetts Book Award

- *The Waters Between Us: A Boy, A Father, Outdoor Misadventures, and the Healing Power of Nature*

- *Until I Have No Country: A Novel of King Philip's Indian War*, Christopher Matthews Publishing

- *King Philip's War: The History and Legacy of America's Forgotten Conflict*, W.W. Norton, coauthor Eric Schultz

- *Above & Beyond: John F. Kennedy and America's Most Dangerous Spy Mission*, PublicAffairs, coauthor Casey Sherman

- *There's a Porcupine in My Outhouse: Misadventures of a Mountain Man Wannabe*, On Cape Publications, winner of the Independent Publishers Association Best Nature Book of the Year Award

- *So Close to Home: A True Story of an American Family's Fight for Survival During WWII*, Pegasus Books, coauthor Alison O'Leary

- *River Days: Exploring the Connecticut River from Source to Sea*, On Cape Publications

- *AMC's Best Day Hikes Near Boston*, Appalachian Mountain Club

- *Nature Walks in Central and Western MA*

- *Exploring the Hidden Charles*

- *Country Roads of Massachusetts*

- *Quiet Places of Massachusetts*

- *New England Wild Places*

- *The Cringe Chronicles* [with Kristin Tougias]

- *Quabbin: A History and Explorers Guide*

- *The Blizzard of '78*

- Middle Reader Books: *The Finest Hours, A Storm Too Soon, Attacked At Sea, Into the Blizzard, Abandon Ship, Claws, and Ghost of the Forest, In Harm's Way* [coauthor Doug Stanton]

# BIBLIOGRAPHY

## CHAPTER 1: THE POWER OF LITTLE STEPS & SURVIVORS' MINDSETS

Author interview with Brad Cavanaugh

Author interview with Ernie Hazard

## CHAPTER 2: THINKING OUTSIDE ONESELF

Author interview with Lochlin Reidy

Alexander, Caroline. *The Bounty*. Viking, 2003

Blackburn, Howard. *The Terrible Odyssey of Howard Blackburn American Heritage*. Feb/March 1982 [republished from Blackburns's 1932 Interview to Salem Evening News]

Bligh, William. *The Bounty Mutiny*. Penguin, 2001

Brokaw, Tom. *Boom*. Random House, 2007

Coakley, Tom. Interview on NPR, 2008.

Creagan, Edward. *How Not to Be My Patient*. Write on Ink Publishing, 2014

Donat, Alexander. *The Holocaust Kingdom*. Holocaust Publishers, 2000

Frankl, Viktor. *Man's Search for Meaning*. Beacon Press, 2006

Garland, Joseph, *Lone Voyager*. Touchstone, 2000

Hirshberg, Caryle. *Remarkable Recoveries*. Riverhead, 1995

Myers, John. *The Saga of Hugh Glass*. Bison Books, 1976

Schuyler, Nick. Interview with Oprah Winfrey. Oprah.com, 2010

Schuyler, Nick. *Not Without Hope*. Harper Collins, 2010

Stanton, Doug. *In Harm's Way*. Owl Books, 2003

## CHAPTER 3: CONTROL, REACTION, DETACH

Byrd, Richard. *Alone*. GP Putnam & Sons, 1938

Franklin, Jonathan. *438 Days*. Atria Books, 2015

Hallums, Roy. *Buried Alive*. Thomas Nelson Publishers, 2010

Racina, Amy. *Angels in the Wilderness*. Elite Books. 2005

"Ex-hostage Recounts Terrible Solitude." *Reuters*, October 27, 2008

## CHAPTER 4: INTUITION

Author Interview Cathy Gilcrest

Bishop, Hugh. *Marblehead's First Harbor*. History Press, 2011

De Becker, Gavin. *The Gift of Fear*. Back Bay Books, 2021

Gigerenzer, Gerd. *Gut Feelings*. Penguin Books, 2008

Junger, Sebastian. *The Perfect Storm*. W.W. Norton, 1997

Kiley, Deborah Scalding. *Albatross*. Houghton Mifflin. 1994

Mayer, Elizabeth Lloyd. *Extraordinary Knowing*. Bantam, 2008

## CHAPTER 5: HELP FROM WITHIN & BEYOND

Author Interview with Bernie Webber

Author Interview Bob Cummings

Author Interview Ernie Hazard

Author Interview Josh Scornavacchi

Author Interview Loch Reidy

Author Interview Ray Downs

Tape Recording from Ina Downs

Baily, Maurice, and Maralyn Baily. *117 Days Adrift*. Nautical, 1974

Byrd, Richard. *Alone*. GP Putman & Sons, 1938

Geiger, John. *The Third Man Factor*. Hachette Books, 2010

Lansing, Alfred. *Endurance*. Basic Books, 2015

Logan, Richard. *Alone*. Stackpole Books, 2018

Parrado, Nando. *Miracle in the Andes*.

Ramsey, Nancy. *Sports Illustrated*, Back from the Brink, January 19, 2004

Simpson, Joe. *Touching the Void*. Perennial, 2004

Whittaker, James. *We Thought We Heard Angels Sing*. E.P. Dutton, 1943

## CHAPTER 6: ENDURING—PEP TALKS, PATS ON THE BACK, & THE POSSIBILITY OF LUCK

Author Interview Lochlin Reidy

Author Interview Ernie Hazard

Baily, Maurice, and Maralyn Baily. *117 Days Adrift*. Nautical, 1974

Douglas Wardrop, Marine Radio Museum [UK] "N/V British Monarch, Wednesday 9th, June 1957"

Morgan, Dodge. *The Voyage of American Promise*. Houghton Mifflin, 1989

Racina, Amy. *Angels in the Wilderness*. Elite Books. 2005

Reeman, Douglas. *Against the Sea*. Hutchinson, 1971

Santoli, Albert. *To Bear Any Burden*. E.P. Dutton, 1985

Wiseman, Richard. *The Luck Factor*. Miramax, 2003

*The Wall Street Journal*, Train Your Brain, August 28, 2012

## CHAPTER 7: RAPID RECOGNITION VS. DENIAL

CBS "Family Under Attack"

Climbing.com, May 5, 2017, "The Push," Tommy Caldwell

Discovery Channel, "Cruise Ship Disaster: Inside the Costa Concordia," 2012

*Newsweek*, February 2, 2009 "What it Takes to Survive a Crisis," Ben Sherwood

*Outside Magazine*, June 1, 2008, Back from the Edge, Greg Child

*People Magazine*, March 3, 2008, "How They Caught a Killer"

Ripley, Amanda. *The Unthinkable*. Harmony, 2009

*Science Magazine*, "Lacking Control Increases Illusory Pattern Perception," Jennifer Whitson and Adam Galinsky

*Star-Ledger*, Katherine Santiago, "Miracle on the Hudson, US Airways Flight 1549 Transcript Released

Tailstrike.com/150109.HTM

## CHAPTER 8: BLINDED BY THE GOAL

Author Interview Bob Cummings & Jerry McCarthy

Heil, Nick. *Dark Summit*. Henry Holt, 2008

Madgic, Bob. *Shattered Air*. Burford Books, 2005

Millard, Candice. *River of Doubt*. Broadway Books, 2006

## CHAPTER 9: QUESTION THE EXPERTS (ESPECIALLY ON VACATION!)

Author Interview with Donald, last name kept private [Bahamas incident]

Mysuncoast.com, North Port Man Who Survived Hang Gliding
    Heads Back for another Try

YouTube, "Swiss Mishap"

## CHAPTER 10: DIGGING DEEP FOR OPTIONS & RESOURCEFULNESS

American Heritage, Survivors America, "A Desperate Trek Across
    America" by Andrés Reséndez

American Heritage, Survivors America, "Disaster at a Distant Moon"
    by Tom Jones

I Survived [interview with John Vihtelic] WROC, January 29, 2012

People in Peril, Readers Digest Association, 1983, Pleasantville,
    NY "The Sixteen-Day Ordeal of John Vihtelic" by Emily and Per
    Ola d'Aulaire

Roberts, David. Alone on the Ice. W.W. Norton, 2013

Rowlandson, Mary. The Narrative of the Captivity and Restoration
    of Mrs. Mary Rowlandson, 1682. Edited by Robert Diebold,
    Lancaster, MA, Town of Lancaster 1975.

## CHAPTER 11: EMOTION, ADRENALINE, AND THE ADVANTAGE OF PAUSING & REVERSIBILITY

Author interview JP de Lutz, Rudy Snell, Ben Tye

Brafman, Rom, and Ori Brafman. Sway. Broadway Books, 2009

Cognitive Processes under Time Stress, Edland, A. 1989, University
    of Stockholm

Hamilton, Diane, Calming Your Brain During Conflict, article in
    Harvard Business Review, Boston, December 22, 2015

Hormone Health Network [hormone.org]

Kennedy, Robert. Thirteen Days. NY, NY. W.W. Norton, 19669

May, Ernest, and Philip Zelikow, *The Kennedy Tapes*, Cambridge MA Harvard University Press, 1997.

Realfirstaid.co.uk

Schlesinger, Arthur, Jr. *A Thousand Days*, Boston, Houghton Mifflin, 1965

Schoen, Marc, and Kristin Loberg *Your Survival Instinct is Killing You*. Plume, 2014

Sherman, Casey, and Michael Tougias, *Above & Beyond*. Public Affairs, NY, NY, 2018

Watkins, Alan PhD. *Coherence*. Kogan Page Publishers, 2021

## CHAPTER 12: FOR AS LONG AS IT TAKES

Author interviews with Scott Higgins, Drew Dazzo, Nevada Smith, Aaron Nelson,

Author interviews with Steve Cerveny and Steve Bonn

Large, Tony. *In Deep and Troubled Waters*. Paul Watkins Publishing, 2001

McCain, John III. *Faith of My Fathers*. Random House, August 1999

US News and World Report, "John McCain; POW, January 28, 2008

## CHAPTER 13: FINAL THOUGHTS

Author Interview Ernie Hazard

Author Interview Loch Reidy

Author Interview Jean Pierre de Lutz

"In a Life and Death Crisis," Sam Walker, Wall Street Journal

Morgan, Dodge. The Voyage of American Promise. Houghton Mifflin, 1989

Mango Publishing, established in 2014, publishes an eclectic list of books by diverse authors—both new and established voices—on topics ranging from business, personal growth, women's empowerment, LGBTQ+ studies, health, and spirituality to history, popular culture, time management, decluttering, lifestyle, mental wellness, aging, and sustainable living. We were recently named 2019 *and* 2020's #1 fastest-growing independent publisher by *Publishers Weekly*. Our success is driven by our main goal, which is to publish high-quality books that will entertain readers as well as make a positive difference in their lives.

Our readers are our most important resource; we value your input, suggestions, and ideas. We'd love to hear from you—after all, we are publishing books for you!

Please stay in touch with us and follow us at:

Facebook: Mango Publishing
Twitter: @MangoPublishing
Instagram: @MangoPublishing
LinkedIn: Mango Publishing
Pinterest: Mango Publishing
Newsletter: mangopublishinggroup.com/newsletter

Join us on Mango's journey to reinvent publishing, one book at a time.

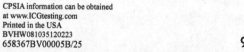

9 781684 810611